THE WOMAN'S DAY BUFFET COOKBOOK

by

Carol Truax

Fawcett Columbine ● **New York**

THE WOMAN'S DAY BUFFET COOKBOOK

Published by Fawcett Columbine Books, CBS Educational and Professional Publishing, a division of CBS Inc.

ISBN: 0-449-90080-0

Photography Credits:
Plates 1, 4, 5, 6 Top by Irwin Horowitz
Plates 7, 8 by Ed Zardowski
Plate 3 by Will Rosseau
Plate 2 by George Torgensen
Plate 6 Bottom by Woman's Day Studio

Printed in the United States of America

Book Club Edition

10 9 8 7 6 5 4 3 2 1

CONTENTS

Menus are for 8 unless otherwise
stated. The recipes in the chapter titled
Fork-Food Buffets are for 10. Your
mathematical skill is all that is required
to obtain the quantity you want.

All gelatin is unflavored unless noted.

INTRODUCTION

In praise of buffets: Whether it is for eight or for eighty, formal or informal, conventional or exotic, there is no better way to serve a meal. In fact, there is often no other way to entertain, in these days of inadequate dining space and insufficient service. Even eight guests, seated at a dining room table, cannot be properly attended to by one person; the meat cools on the plate before the last vegetable is able to join it...and this problem is compounded geometrically when the number of guests multiplies.

These difficulties do not exist with a buffet, at which the entire meal can be presented beautifully. Equally important for the hostess, most of the dishes can be partially or entirely prepared in advance. The whole menu, handsomely displayed, will greet the eyes of each approaching guest, who is free to indulge his or her own taste. Something one doesn't care for or shouldn't eat can be avoided without embarrassment, and the size of portions is governed entirely by one's desire. As a result, clean plates become the rule, and unwanted food remains untouched on the platter, and can be frozen for use another day.

The success of a buffet depends not only on the meal itself but on the handling of details. With a little foresight, all the nightmares can be avoided; the long line scarcely moving because there is no place to put one's plate while using two hands on a complicated platter, or there are too many alternatives to choose from; meanwhile, the bewildered guests mill around trying to find a place to sit down.

Use a sideboard, buffet or long table, keeping the flow of traffic in mind. Your floral centerpieces, unlike those at a sit-down dinner, need not be low: tall blossoms form a colorful background. Small plants at each end of the table are unusual and effective. Fruit makes an excellent centerpiece: red apples, green and dark grapes, or, best of all, a basket or low bowl overflowing with assorted fruits. This can double for dessert, especially when augmented by a tray of various cheeses. Lighted candles add glamour to the food—and to the guests.

The size of your table should regulate the number of dishes you offer. Don't clutter the space, but remember to provide more variety than you would at a formal dinner. Arrange the platters in logical sequence, keeping in mind the total picture, including form and color. Be sure to leave room for the guest to rest his plate. Silver, napkins and stacked plates must be conveniently located at the beginning of the buffet.

If there is room for it, a salad bar will be a stellar attraction. Use a separate table or—less desirable—the end of the buffet itself. Guests should be able to take their time without holding up the line. Similarly, there can be a dessert bar offering goodies in its own environment. After-dinner coffee should be served when the guests are finished eating. It does not belong on the buffet, but should be passed or separately set up.

Sitting together at a large table is the best way to enjoy a meal. Smaller tables are adequate; card tables will seat four or, with the addition of a round top, six or eight. Individual tables are satisfactory and are not too costly, either in nests or the folding type. Last of all comes the lap, which is preferable only to standing. For large groups, folding chairs may be necessary.

There is also the semi-buffet, which combines the best of two possible worlds. A first course, usually cold, awaits the guests at their designated places at table, or it may be served to them with the aperitifs, thus covering the gap between the prompt and the tardy arrivals. The dessert course may be served after the main part of the meal. A semi-buffet can avoid confusion without requiring much assistance.

When it is not possible to provide sufficient table space, the fork-food meal is essential, as food simply cannot be cut up while balancing a plate on one's lap. Fortunately, there are a great many excellent dishes such as casseroles, curries, seafoods, and meal salads, which feature bite-sized pieces.

Although hot buffets include some cold items, such as a salad, the emphasis is upon the main dish—or dishes, for with a buffet, one need not gear one's pièce de résistance to the least common gastronomic denominator, but can provide a simple back-up entrée for the fussy eater. Hot buffet menus are similar to those of traditional dinners, except for a somewhat larger number of dishes.

Luncheon buffets are practically identical with dinners, except that the number of items is usually reduced, and the lighter ones are selected.

Brunch is a different matter. Traditionally served as a buffet, it is a combination of lunch and breakfast, featuring dishes appropriate to the latter.

The cold buffet is not only a delight in hot weather, but a boon to the hostess who, having attended a concert or some other entertainment, can return home with her guests and find "a thing of beauty" ready and waiting. It is also a way to avoid the problems posed by latecomers.

The buffet is convenient, convivial and lovely to look at, but in the final analysis, it is only as good as its food, as good as each individual dish, and the combination of dishes that constitute the meal. If you follow the menus and the recipes in this book, your buffet will be very good indeed.

PLANNING A BUFFET

Preparing food ahead is the secret of a successful hostess! There is no difficulty if you plan your menu carefully to cook in advance. There are dishes that can be made days ahead and frozen, others to do the night before and many the morning of the party. Marketing can almost always be done a day or two before the event. Your kitchen may be small or you may have work to do so take advantage of recipes which are improved by being cooked and then reheated. Stews and casseroles, for example, have a better flavor after reheating. Food steamed in foil may also be refrigerated in its foil package and baked according to directions with no attention until serving time. Vegetables can all be cleaned in advance, even those that need last minute cooking. Most desserts lend themselves to advance preparation and many actually have to be done in advance. Salad greens and some of the other ingredients can be washed way ahead and kept crisp until ready to assemble. Small salads can be built ahead with an already made dressing added just before serving.

BUFFET TABLE DECORATING

Flowers are always lovely on a dinner or buffet table. For the buffet a long narrow arrangement fits well. The flowers can be higher than on a dining table where one doesn't wish to dodge the flowers to look at neighbors across the way. Fruit is very versatile. As a centerpiece it is not only colorful but also can double for dessert, especially if it is accompanied by a cheese tray. There are many to choose from, in combination or singly; a bowl of red apples with a few green leaves tucked in; a bowl of grapes, perhaps of different colors; or an assortment of various colored fruits can be a work of art.

A piece of china or pottery such as a soup tureen is easy and attractive. A plant or perhaps a pair of small plants, flowering or green, will live somewhere else in the house later on so it is not an extravagance. There are many things to choose from.

CALENDAR OF PREPARATION

Set the buffet table the night before or day of the party at your leisure. Fix the flowers or other centerpiece the day of the buffet. Get out serving dishes, platters, and serving pieces the day of the dinner. If white wine is to be served, chill it and place it on the buffet just before serving. Serve red wine at room temperature. Set up your bar, if you are serving drinks ahead, and be sure you have enough ice.

Get dressed and relax!

LUNCHEONS, SUPPERS, TEAS, COCKTAILS AND PARTIES

Luncheons can be derived from the menus of hot or cold buffets. You will want 2 or 3 less items and the dishes should be the lighter ones. Meal salads are especially appropriate.

The late supper easily descends from cold buffets. Of course, neither luncheons nor suppers are limited to cold. Suppers often follow an event of some sort and should not take too long to eat. They should have few courses, which should be tempting and not heavy or hearty.

The tea, and its afternoon relations, differs from dinner buffets in that everything is displayed on a table, around which the guests gather. This is the time for your finest tea service, your best linen and china and your most attractive centerpiece. Candles and flowers are almost a requirement; they should be appropriate to the season, the occasion and the decor. Tea and coffee are traditional, but you may wish to serve other beverages as well. Handsome platters of dainty sandwiches, cookies and small cakes and small plates of candies round out the picture.

Cocktail parties center about the bar, which may be on the table. It should be completely fitted with glasses of assorted size, liquor, mixes, water and ice. Cocktail canapés should be plentiful, easy to reach and to eat. Serve a few hot as well as cold ones, also perhaps some cheese and crackers and bowls of nuts and crunchies. Cocktail napkins are necessary, paper or real. However, it is not important to have enough chairs to go around, since many people prefer to stand.

BRUNCHES

Brunch is a horrid word for a nice meal—a combination of breakfast and lunch, usually served in the late morning. The dishes are less varied than at luncheon and they suggest a breakfast; such as assorted breads, rolls and coffee cake, eggs, bacon, ham, sausages, as well as mushrooms and fried chicken, chicken livers and kidneys. There are many dishes to choose from. You don't really need desserts unless you wish to serve fruit or a berry pie to New Englanders. You *do* need to serve coffee with the meal.

Sunday or Holiday Brunches. Choose a number of dishes from the following:

Juices: Orange, grapefruit, tomato, V-8, pine-apple, apple

Fruits: Grapefruit, melon, sliced oranges, berries

Breads: Toast, muffins, biscuits, popovers*, croissants, brioche, corn bread*, cinnamon rolls, coffeecake
Jam, marmalade, jelly

Scrambled eggs and variations: Herb, tomato, cheese, ham, Canadian bacon, sausages, kidneys*, chicken livers*, corned beef hash, chicken hash*, finnan haddie*, kippered herring, codfish cakes*, trout*

A slightly less elaborate brunch may be served any day of the week.

*See Index

MENUS

You do not have to follow menus without making changes. Many vegetables are seasonal and you can adjust accordingly. The suggested menus are to show foods appropriate to serve together. Do not change the balance of the meal, which has been carefully selected with an eye to vegetables, starches and protein as well as color and texture. This balance has been maintained with vegetarian menus, which offer unusual meatless recipes.

I

THE SEMI-BUFFET

If you have space to seat your guests at table, but inadequate help to serve them properly, the practice of having the first course at the table, and then going to the buffet, is most satisfactory. Tables are prepared as they would be at a sit-down dinner: place cards, silver, napkins and glasses. The first course is also awaiting the guests. This is usually cold, but need not be; for example, hot soup can be ladled at the table.

The main course, hot and tempting, is on the buffet, while the desserts may be at table, on the buffet or on a separate dessert bar. For a larger party, the first course may be canapés, both hot and cold, served with the aperitif in the living room. Either way you have only the main course to contend with at the buffet. Advantages: You know where you will sit; you have begun conversations and will have to get up only once. You are then off to a good start for an excellent dinner.

SEMI-BUFFET

Melon
Baked Ham
Mustard Sauce
Pan-Fried Chicken
Scalloped Potatoes
Spinach Ring with Mushrooms
Cooked Vegetable Salad II
Melba Toast
Spanish Cream
Meringues

BAKED HAM

1 (12–14 pound) ready-to-eat ham
1½ cups brown sugar
Whole cloves

½ cup cider
Candied cherries (optional)

Trim most of the skin off the ham, leaving it on the shank end. Rub with half the brown sugar. Score the fat and insert cloves. Bake at 325° F. for 30 minutes. Baste with the remaining sugar mixed with cider and cook 30 minutes longer. Decorate with the cherries, if you wish. Serves 14 to 16.

MUSTARD SAUCE

2 tablespoons dry mustard
½ cup brown or white sugar
¼ teaspoon salt
1 teaspoon flour

¼ cup broth or water with a bouillon
  cube, cold or hot
¼ cup vinegar
1 egg, beaten

Mix the dry ingredients in the top of a double boiler. Stir in the broth and vinegar. Add the egg and cook and stir until thickened. Cool. Excellent with cold fish. Yield: about 1 cup.

PAN-FRIED CHICKEN

Chicken does not have to be Southern fried, deep fried, coated with batter to be good—here are two ways.

2 3-pound chickens
1 cup flour
1½ teaspoons salt

½ teaspoon pepper
½ teaspoon paprika
½ cup oil or shortening

Have the chickens cut into serving pieces. Shake a few pieces at a time in a paper bag with mixture of flour, salt, pepper and paprika. Heat the oil or shortening and fry the chicken for about 20 minutes. Turn and brown on the other side for 15 minutes. Be careful not to burn the chicken; it should be evenly browned. Drain in paper toweling. Keep warm in the oven until ready to serve.

OVEN-FRIED CHICKEN

Prepare the chicken as for Pan-Fried Chicken (see preceding recipe). Brush with melted butter. Place on a greased baking pan and bake at 375° F. for 40 minutes, turning the pieces once.

SCALLOPED POTATOES

6 or 7 large potatoes
⅓ to ½ cup butter
2 small onions, sliced very thin
    (optional)
1 teaspoon salt

½ teaspoon pepper, preferably white
3 tablespoons flour
Half-and-half or milk
Dry bread crumbs (optional)

Peel the potatoes and slice very thin. Butter a 2½-quart casserole and put a layer of potatoes in the bottom. Sprinkle with onions, if you wish, and a third of the salt, pepper and flour. Dot with 1 tablespoon butter. Repeat, making 3 more layers, ending with potatoes on top. Pour in half-and-half or milk to cover the potatoes completely. Bake at 400° F. for about 1 hour, or until quite tender. You may brown under the broiler for a few minutes, if you wish. Also you may cover the top with ¼ cup dry bread crumbs and dot with butter; if you use crumbs, brown them under the broiler.

SPINACH RING WITH MUSHROOMS

¾ cup milk
2 eggs, beaten
1 teaspoon salt
¼ teaspoon pepper
¼ teaspoon nutmeg

6 tablespoons butter
5 cups finely chopped, drained,
    cooked spinach (3 10-ounce
    packages frozen or 2 pounds fresh)
2 pounds mushrooms, sliced

Scald the milk and blend with the eggs. Add the salt, pepper, nutmeg, and 2 tablespoons of the butter. Stir until the butter melts. Add the spinach, mix well and adjust seasoning. Pour into a well-greased, 6-cup ring mold and bake in a pan of water in a 350° F. oven for about 40 minutes, or until set. Meanwhile, sauté the mushrooms for 2 minutes in the remaining 4 tablespoons butter and keep warm. Before serving, loosen the edges of the mold with a spatula and turn out into a platter. Fill the center of the ring with the mushrooms.

COOKED VEGETABLE SALAD II

4 large carrots, scraped and diced
½ pound green beans, cut into ½-inch lengths
1 small head cauliflower, cut into small flowerets

1 10-ounce package frozen green peas, or 1 pound fresh
½ pound mushrooms, caps and stems cut into thick slices
½ cup French Dressing (see page 155 for recipe)

Cook the carrots and beans in a steamer over hot water in a tightly covered pot for 5 minutes. Add the cauliflower and peas and cook for 5 minutes. If using frozen peas, cook separately according to package instructions and drain. Add mushrooms to the vegetables and cook for 3 minutes. Cool. Add the drained cooked frozen peas. Drain off any excess liquid and chill. Add French Dressing, toss and chill for several hours. Serves 8 to 10.

SPANISH CREAM

3 cups milk
1 envelope gelatin
⅛ teaspoon salt
½ cup sugar
3 eggs, separated

1 teaspoon vanilla
1 tablespoon sherry
Whipped or plain cream or pureed fruits (optional)

Pour the milk into the top of a double boiler and soften the gelatin in it for 5 minutes. Place over hot water and add the salt and sugar, stirring until they are dissolved. Gradually stir into the slightly beaten egg yolks, return the mixture to the double boiler and cook until slightly thickened, stirring constantly. Remove from heat, pour into a bowl and add the vanilla and the sherry. Fold in the stiffly beaten egg whites. Turn into a wet bowl or mold and chill. Turn out on a platter to serve with or without cream, whipped cream or pureed fruits.

MERINGUES

3 egg whites
⅛ teaspoon salt

1 cup sugar
½ teaspoon vanilla

Beat the egg whites and salt until frothy. Add the sugar, a tablespoon at a time. Beat until the meringue will stand in stiff peaks and the sugar is dissolved. Fold in the vanilla. Drop by teaspoonfuls onto a greased baking sheet. Bake at 275° F. for about 1 hour or until light tan. Let dry in oven. Yield: 2½ dozen.

SEMI-BUFFET

Mussels on the Half Shell
Turkey in Foil, with Stuffing
Apricot Puree
Noodle Salad with Ham
Braised Celery
Brussels Sprouts
Wilted Lettuce
Chocolate Cheesecake

MUSSELS ON THE HALF SHELL WITH LEMON

4 to 6 dozen medium to large mussels
6 tablespoons olive oil
3 tablespoons lemon juice

1 teaspoon pepper
2 tablespoons minced parsley

If you can open the mussels with a knife, do so. Otherwise, cut beards from mussels and steam the debearded mussels for only 1 or 2 minutes and remove at once from the pot. You want them only to open, not cook. Chill the mussels. Pull the top shell from each and leave the mussel in the bottom shell. Place on 8 plates. Combine the remaining ingredients. Mix and spread over the mussels. Chill.

TURKEY IN FOIL, WITH STUFFING

Pat the turkey dry inside and out with paper towels. Sprinkle with salt and fill with stuffing, if you wish. Brush with a little butter and place on a piece of foil large enough to cover the bird. Wrap securely, closing the foil tight so that no juice can escape. Roast at 400° F. for 2½ hours for a 10- to 12-pound turkey; 3 hours for a 14- to 16-pound turkey; 4 hours for an 18- to 20-pound turkey. Open the foil for the last 40 to 60 minutes of cooking to brown the skin. Lift onto a platter and let it "rest" for 30 minutes before carving. Make

13

gravy from the defatted juices from the foil by stirring in 2 tablespoons of flour and ½ cup boiling water. Simmer until thick and smooth. Add more water if too thick. Use Bread Stuffing or Rice Stuffing (see below for recipes).

BREAD STUFFING

½ cup butter or margarine	½ teaspoon pepper
1 cup chopped onion	1½ teaspoons poultry seasoning
1 cup finely diced celery	3 quarts firm-type bread crumbs, or 2
1 teaspoon salt	1-pound loaves bread, cubed

Melt butter or margarine in small skillet or saucepan. Add onion and celery and cook, stirring frequently, for about 5 minutes. Add seasonings and cook about 3 minutes longer. Add to bread and toss well. Enough for a 12-pound turkey.

Egg-Bread Stuffing: Beat 2 eggs slightly and add to stuffing with the crumbs.

RICE STUFFING

1 cup chopped celery	½ teaspoon marjoram
½ cup chopped onion	1 teaspoon tarragon or thyme
¼ cup butter	½ teaspoon salt
6 cups cooked white or brown rice	¼ teaspoon pepper

Sauté the celery and onion in butter until light brown. Add the rice and seasonings and stir and cook for a few minutes. Spoon loosely into the cavities of the bird. This will stuff 1 8-pound turkey, or 2 4-pound chickens.

APRICOT PUREE

1 1-pound 4-ounce can peeled apricots, seeded	Grated peel of 1 lemon
1 tablespoon lemon juice	

Puree the apricots with lemon juice and peel in a blender or processor. Serve at room temperature. Especially good with turkey or veal. Yield: 1½ cups.

NOODLE SALAD WITH HAM

(color plate 5)

6 cups chicken broth	1 cup frozen green peas
1 8-ounce box egg noodles, or 8 ounces loose or homemade	1 cup shredded romaine or spinach
¾ pound thinly sliced ham, cut in strips (about 1 cup)	1 teaspoon soy sauce
	2 scallions, sliced

In large saucepan bring broth to boil. Add noodles, cover and simmer for 10 minutes. Add remaining ingredients except scallions and cook just until heated through. Sprinkle with scallions.

BRAISED CELERY

3 small or 2 large heads celery
¼ cup butter
1 to 2 cups chicken or beef broth or
    water with bouillon cubes

Salt
½ cup slivered almonds (optional)

Remove the leaves and cut the celery into 3-inch pieces. Brown in the butter. Add broth almost to cover and simmer for about 15 minutes, or until tender. Transfer the celery into a warm serving dish and reduce the liquid to about 1 cup. Add salt to taste. Pour over the celery. If you use the almonds, sauté them in an additional 2 tablespoons butter and add the cooking liquid to them before reducing it. Serves 6.

BRUSSELS SPROUTS

2 pounds brussels sprouts or 3
    10-ounce packages frozen
1 teaspoon salt

3 tablespoons melted butter
½ pound chestnuts, peeled and sliced
    (optional)

Steam or cook the sprouts in a very small amount of water for 10 to 12 minutes until crisp-tender. Season with salt and butter. You may add the chestnuts, if you wish.

WILTED LETTUCE

3 slices bacon
1 medium-sized onion, chopped fine
2 tablespoons water
2 tablespoons vinegar

½ teaspoon salt
¼ teaspoon pepper
1 tablespoon sugar
1 head iceberg lettuce, or 1 pound
    spinach leaves

Cook the bacon until crisp. Remove and place on paper towels. Sauté the onion in bacon drippings until transparent not brown. Add water, vinegar, salt, pepper and sugar and keep hot. Put the lettuce or spinach in a bowl and pour the hot bacon drippings over, scraping all the onion onto the lettuce. Toss. Serve with the crisp bacon crumbled over the top.

WILTED CABBAGE

Substitute 1 medium-sized head shredded cabbage for the lettuce or spinach and return the whole salad to the pan. Heat for a few minutes until the cabbage is wilted.

CHOCOLATE CHEESECAKE

3 8-ounce packages cream cheese, at
  room temperature
1 teaspoon vanilla
⅛ teaspoon salt
1 cup sugar
12 ounces semisweet chocolate (2
  cups chocolate pieces or 12
  squares), melted and cooled

3 eggs
1 cup sour cream
Chocolate Crust (see page 157 for
  recipe)
Whipped cream (optional)

In large bowl beat cream cheese until smooth. Add vanilla, salt and sugar, beating until very smooth. Add chocolate and beat until well blended. Add eggs, one at a time, scraping bowl and beating well after each. Add sour cream and beat until smooth. Spoon into crumb crust (in springform pan), smooth top and bake at 375° F. for 1 hour (cake will still be soft). Cool completely on rack. Leave in pan, cover top with foil, and refrigerate overnight. With sharp, heavy knife cut around sides of crust, pressing knife blade firmly against pan. Release and remove sides of pan. Insert firm (not flexible) metal spatula gently under crust; ease around to release cake completely from bottom of pan. Cake can be refrigerated, or frozen if you wish. Place on large flat platter. Serve cold with garnished whipped cream. Serves 14.

SEMI-BUFFET

Chinese food is ideal for a buffet.

Wonton Soup
Shrimp-Pork Egg Rolls
Vegetable Chop Suey
Chinese Chicken
Steak Kew with Broccoli
Steamed Rice
Tea Eggs
Almond Cookies
Kumquats (on toothpicks)
Tea

WONTON SOUP

(color plate 3)

5 cups chicken broth
2 cups water
2 tablespoons soy sauce
16 small wontons

¼ pound cooked ham or pork, cut in
thin strips
2 scallions, chopped

In large saucepan bring broth, water and soy sauce to boil. Add wontons and cook for about 5 minutes, or until heated through. Add ham or pork and scallions. Serve hot.

SHRIMP-PORK EGG ROLLS

(color plate 3)

6 cups shredded cabbage (1½ pounds)
6 cups thinly sliced celery (about 12 ribs)
Oil
1 pound ground lean pork (about 2 cups)
1 cup chopped scallions
1 cup chopped cooked shrimp (about ½ pound)

2 tablespoons soy sauce, or to taste
1 tablespoon Oriental sesame oil (optional)
½ teaspoon pepper
Salt to taste
12 egg roll skins, or 6 purchased
1 egg white

In a large pot combine cabbage, celery and enough water to cover. Bring to boil, and cook for about 5 minutes, or until tender. Drain in colander, then cool. Press vegetables against side of colander to extract liquid. Vegetables should look dry. In large skillet heat 2 tablespoons oil until very hot but not smoking. Stir-fry pork, breaking up meat with a spoon, about 5 minutes, or until it loses its pinkness. Add scallions and stir-fry for 1 minute. Remove skillet from heat. Stir in vegetables, shrimp, soy sauce, sesame oil, pepper and salt. Mix well, then set aside to cool. To assemble: with one corner of egg roll skin pointing toward you, place ½ cup filling slightly below center. Fold up bottom corner to cover filling, then fold over left and right corners. Firmly roll skin away from you. Brush top corner with egg white, press to seal like a flap, making sure filling is securely wrapped. In deep fat fryer or large saucepan heat 4 cups oil to 375° F. Add 3 egg rolls at a time and fry until crisp and golden. Remove with slotted spoon or tongs and drain on paper towels (do not stack egg rolls while warm since they will lose crispness). Serve hot.

NOTE: To freeze egg rolls, fry only until pale golden. Drain on paper towels, cool. Wrap airtight. Freeze up to 1 month. Before serving, thaw, then bake at 375° F. for 20 minutes, or until hot, or fry in deep fat 1 to 2 minutes, or until golden brown.

VEGETABLE CHOP SUEY

2 tablespoons butter
4 cups coarsely shredded cabbage
2 cups thinly sliced celery
2 cups sliced green pepper

½ cup thinly sliced onion
1 teaspoon salt
¼ teaspoon pepper
3 tablespoons soy sauce

In a large skillet melt the butter and add the cabbage, celery, pepper and onion. Cover and cook over low heat for 5 minutes. Season with salt, pepper and soy sauce. Cook, uncovered, for 1 minute longer, stirring gently. Serves 10 to 12.

CHINESE CHICKEN

2 3- to 3½-pound frying chickens, boned and chopped into 2-inch pieces
1 tablespoon cornstarch

2 tablespoons soy sauce
2 tablespoons sherry or rice wine
3 scallions, chopped fine
2 teaspoons chopped ginger

Put the chicken in a bowl or deep platter. Combine the remaining ingredients and spread over the chicken. Steam on the rack of a steamer for 40 minutes. Serve in the dish it was steamed in.

CHINESE CHICKEN WITH MUSHROOMS

Soak ¼ pound dried Chinese mushrooms in water to cover half an hour. Then slice and add to Chinese Chicken before steaming. You may add 1 6-ounce can water chestnuts, sliced, if you wish.

STEAK KEW WITH BROCCOLI

(color plate 3)

1½ pounds lean flank or round steak
4 cups oil
1 tablespoon minced ginger root
2 cloves garlic, minced
¼ cup catsup
2 tablespoons hoisin sauce (if available)
2 tablespoons dry sherry

3 tablespoons soy sauce
1 tablespoon sugar
1½ bunches broccoli (about 2 pounds)
½ cup chopped scallions
⅓ cup chicken broth
3 tablespoons cornstarch blended with ¼ cup water

Score beef on both sides across the grain. Cut in 1-inch cubes. Set aside in medium-sized bowl. In small saucepan heat 2 tablespoons of the oil until very hot but not smoking. Add ginger root and garlic and stir over high heat for 30 seconds. Stir in catsup, hoisin sauce, sherry, 2 tablespoons of the soy sauce and sugar. Pour over beef and toss to coat. Cover and refrigerate for 2 hours or up to 2 days. Slice broccoli lengthwise into 6-inch spears. Place in large skillet with enough water to cover. Bring to boil and cook for 5 minutes, or until tender, then drain. Place on serving dish and keep warm. In small saucepan heat 1 tablespoon oil until very hot but not smoking. Add scallions and stir 30 seconds. Add broth, cornstarch mixture and remaining soy sauce; stir until sauce thickens. Pour over broccoli and keep warm. In deep-fat fryer or large saucepan heat remaining oil to 350° F. Fry a few pieces of beef at a time for 1 to 2 minutes, or until golden. Remove with slotted spoon and drain on paper towels. Place on broccoli.

STEAMED RICE

2½ cups long-grain rice   1 teaspoon salt
2 tablespoons butter   5 cups water

Put the rice in a skillet with the butter and remaining ingredients, cover tightly and steam for 15 to 20 minutes or until the rice is tender when you crush a grain between your fingers. Rake into a warm serving dish with a fork; a spoon will crush some of the grains of rice. Serves 8 to 12.

TEA EGGS

(color plate 3)

10 eggs   ⅓ cup soy sauce
3 tea bags   1 teaspoon anise seed

In 2-quart saucepan place eggs in water to cover; bring to boil and simmer for 10 minutes. Remove eggs with slotted spoon and reserve water. Cool eggs thoroughly in cold water. Gently crack, but do not remove shells. Return eggs to water, bring to boil. Add tea bags, soy sauce and anise seed. Cover and simmer for 1 hour. Drain eggs, cool and remove shells. To store, place eggs in cold water to cover; refrigerate several days (changing water daily).

ALMOND COOKIES

(color plate 3)

1 cup butter or margarine, softened   2½ cups flour
1 cup sugar   1½ teaspoons baking powder
1 egg, beaten   Dash of salt
3 ounces (½ cup) ground blanched   36 whole blanched almonds
    almonds
1 teaspoon almond extract

In large bowl cream butter or margarine with sugar. Beat in egg, ground almonds and extract. Stir together flour, baking powder and salt. Gradually stir into butter mixture. Shape in a ball. Roll out ¼-inch thick between sheets of lightly floured waxed paper. Cut out cookies with a 2½-inch round cookie cutter; reroll scraps. Place about 1 inch apart on greased cookie sheet. Press an almond in center of each. Bake at 350° F. 10 to 12 minutes, or until pale golden. Remove to racks. Yield: about 36 cookies.

SEMI-BUFFET

Cheese Quiche
Whole Fish in Foil
Coq Au Vin
Fettucine
Whole Carrots
Stuffed Cucumbers
Festive Strawberry Sponge Cake

CHEESE QUICHE

2 cups ricotta cheese
½ pound blue cheese (Stilton,
    Gorgonzola or Roquefort),
    crumbled
6 eggs

½ cup heavy cream
1 tablespoon minced parsley
Dash of cayenne
2 10-inch pie shells (prebaked for 10
    minutes)

Mix all ingredients well except pie shells. Turn into preheated shell. Bake at 400° F. for 25 to 30 minutes, or until firm and puffy. Serve warm. Serves 8 to 10.

WHOLE FISH IN FOIL

1 4-pound fish: bass, bluefish,
    snapper, scrod or lake trout
2 teaspoons salt
½ teaspoon pepper
¼ head soft lettuce (Boston, Bibb,
    Leaf, Garden, Escarole, Chicory—
    not Iceberg or Romaine)

2 tablespoons butter
2 or 3 scallions, slivered
Melted butter
Lemon wedges

Place the fish (leaving on the head and tail) on a sheet of foil large enough to wrap it up in. Sprinkle inside and out with salt and pepper. Add the lettuce leaves, butter and scallions.

Wrap the fish envelope fashion so no juices can escape. Bake at 350° F. for about 45 minutes. You can easily roll the fish onto a warm platter, juices and all. Or, place it on a platter to serve, pushing the foil down on the sides. Serve with melted butter and lemon wedges.

BROWNED WHOLE FISH

Proceed as for Whole Fish in Foil, turning the oven up to 500° F. and opening the foil for the last 10 minutes of cooking.

COQ AU VIN

3 3-pound chickens, cut into serving pieces
2 tablespoons oil
¼ cup butter melted
1 medium to large onion, minced
1 teaspoon salt
¼ teaspoon pepper
2 tablespoons minced parsley
2 stalks celery, chopped
2 lemons, cut up
3 cups white or red wine
Sugar
2 tablespoons flour
1 cup chicken broth
24 small white onions, boiled
1 pound mushroom caps (optional)

Brown the chicken in the oil and 2 tablespoons of the butter. Transfer to a casserole. Brown the onion and add to the chicken with the salt, pepper, parsley, celery and lemon. Pour in the wine (adding 1 teaspoon of sugar if using red wine, ½ teaspoon if white). Cook, covered, for 30 to 40 minutes, or until the chicken is tender. Stir the flour into the remaining butter. Add the broth and cook and stir until thickened. Pour over the chicken. Add the white onions and heat together. Add the mushrooms for the last 10 minutes of cooking, if you wish. You may bake this casserole about 45 minutes in a 350° F. oven if you wish. Serves 12.

FETTUCINE

1½ pounds fettucine, fini (fine fettucine)
4 tablespoons minced parsley
1 tablespoon chopped fresh oregano, or 1 teaspoon dried
1 large clove garlic, minced
1 teaspoon salt
¼ cup grated Parmesan cheese
2 tablespoons butter
½ cup tomato puree

Cook the fettucine in a large pot of salted boiling water for about 5 minutes. Drain. Stir in the parsley, oregano, garlic, salt, cheese, butter and tomato puree, blending well. Reheat.

WHOLE CARROTS

3 bunches young carrots or 3 1-pound cans whole
1 tablespoon salt
2 tablespoons minced onion
⅓ cup butter
½ cup light brown sugar
2 teaspoons lemon juice
Grated peel of 1 lemon

If using fresh carrots, scrape them and cook in a tightly covered pot with a little water and ½ teaspoon of the salt or cook on the rack of a steamer. Cook only until crisp-tender but not soft. If canned, drain and boil the liquid to reduce it to about ¼ cup. Sauté the onion for a few minutes in butter until light brown. Add sugar, lemon juice and peel and the remaining 2 teaspoons salt. Heat and stir until the sugar is dissolved. Pour in about ¼ cup of liquid from the carrots. Add the carrots and heat for 5 minutes.

STUFFED CUCUMBERS

4 cucumbers, cut in half lengthwise
½ cup cottage cheese
3 tablespoons minced celery
3 tablespoons minced scallions

1 teaspoon salt
3 tablespoons Mayonnaise (see page 154 for recipe)
Minced chives (garnish)

Scrape the seeds from the center of the cucumbers and mix with the remaining ingredients, except chives. Taste for seasoning and refill the cucumbers. Chill. Serve on the half shell, garnished with chives.

FESTIVE STRAWBERRY SPONGE CAKE

Cake:

1 cup flour
1 teaspoon baking powder
5 eggs
¾ cup sugar
3 tablespoons butter or margarine

¼ cup heavy cream
2 teaspoons grated lemon peel
1 teaspoon lemon extract
1 teaspoon vanilla

Filling and topping:

1 quart strawberries, hulled and halved (reserve a few whole and unhulled for garnish)

½ cup sugar
1½ cups heavy cream, whipped

Cake:

Mix flour and baking powder and set aside. In large bowl on high speed beat eggs and sugar for about 10 minutes, or until lemon-colored, fluffy and thickened. Meanwhile, in small saucepan over low heat melt butter in cream; set aside to cool slightly. Divide batter evenly between 2 well-greased and floured 9-inch layer cake pans. Bake at 350° F. for 22 to 25 minutes. Remove from pans and cool thoroughly on racks.

Filling and topping:

Gently toss berries with sugar. Let stand at room temperature until they draw juice, about 1 hour. Place one cake layer on a serving plate. Spoon half the berries and juice over; top with all but 1 cup whipped cream. Place remaining cake layer on cream and press down lightly. Spoon remaining berries and juice on cake; mound remaining whipped cream in center. Garnish with whole berries. Serves 10.

SEMI-BUFFET

Spinach Soup
Leg of Lamb
Spareribs
Brochette of Swordfish
Flageolets (available in jars or cans)
Applesauce
Glazed Carrots
Mushroom-Celery Salad
Devil's Food Cake

SPINACH SOUP

2 small onions, minced (about ½ cup)
2 tablespoons butter
4 tablespoons flour
4 cups chicken broth

2 pounds spinach, stems removed and
    finely shredded (8 packed cups)
2 cups milk
½ teaspoon salt
Dash of hot pepper sauce (optional)

In a heavy pot over medium heat cook onion in butter, stirring, for about 5 minutes, or until tender but not brown. Blend in flour and cook for 1 minute. Gradually add broth, stirring until thickened and smooth. Add spinach, cover and simmer for 5 minutes, or until wilted and tender. Stir in milk and seasonings. Heat through. If you prefer a smoother soup, process in a blender or a processor. Serves 8 to 10.

LEG OF LAMB

1 6- to 7-pound leg of lamb
1 to 2 cloves garlic, slivered

1 teaspoon salt
1 teaspoon rosemary

Wipe the lamb with a damp cloth. Make slits in the meat with a small sharp knife and insert the slivers of garlic. Mix the salt and rosemary and rub it into the lamb. Roast in an open pan in a 400° F. oven for 1 hour. Turn off the oven and leave the lamb for 15 minutes. It should be pink inside (165° F. to 170° on a meat thermometer for rare to medium rare). It is a shame to cook legs of lamb well done. Serves 8 to 10.

SPARERIBS

(color plate 2)

2 sides pork spareribs (about 8 to 9 pounds)	3 tablespoons Worcestershire sauce
2 teaspoons salt	2 teaspoons prepared mustard
½ teaspoon pepper	1 clove garlic, crushed
1 cup brown sugar	Green Bean Salad or watercress (garnish)
¼ cup vinegar	

Have the spareribs split and cut into 3-inch pieces. Sprinkle with half the salt and pepper. Place in a shallow roasting pan and bake at 350° F. for 30 minutes. Brush with a mixture of the remaining ingredients except garnish, turn and brush again. Bake for 1 hour longer, basting several times. Garnish serving with green bean salad (see page 103 for recipe) or watercress.

BROCHETTE OF SWORDFISH

3-4 pounds of swordfish, cut into 1-inch cubes	½ teaspoon salt
Juice of 1 lemon	⅛ teaspoon pepper
1 teaspoon minced onion	⅛ teaspoon paprika
3 tablespoons oil	1 bay leaf
	8 slices bacon, cut into 1-inch squares

If using frozen fish, thaw it. Put the fish cubes in a bowl with the remaining ingredients, except bacon, and marinate for 1 to 2 hours, turning, to coat on all sides. When ready to cook, string the swordfish on skewers with squares of bacon between the pieces. Brush with the marinade and broil for 5 minutes close to the heat. Turn, brush again with remaining marinade and broil 5 minutes longer. Pour any remaining juices over the fish. Good with rice.

APPLESAUCE

4 pounds cooking apples	1 teaspoon lemon juice
1 cup water	½ teaspoon nutmeg
½ cup sugar	

Peel, core and cut the apples into pieces. Simmer with the remaining ingredients for about 20 minutes, or until the apples are soft. Puree in a blender or processor. Let cool to room temperature before serving.

GLAZED CARROTS

Proceed as for Whole Carrots (see page 22 for recipe). Add 2 tablespoons honey or sugar to the butter and pour over the carrots.

MUSHROOM-CELERY SALAD

1 pound small white mushrooms
1 large head celery, scraped
½ cup olive oil
2 tablespoons lemon juice

1 teaspoon salt
¼ teaspoon pepper
Bibb or Boston lettuce

Wipe the mushrooms and pull the caps from the stems. You'll need very fresh mushrooms. Slice the caps thinly into crescent-shaped pieces. Wash the celery, pull the stalks apart and cut each stalk into slices the same thickness as the mushrooms. They will be similar in shape. Mix gently with the mushrooms. Blend the oil, lemon juice, salt and pepper. Toss carefully with the salad and chill. Serve on the lettuce.

DEVIL'S FOOD CAKE

(with white seven-minute frosting and chocolate curls)

1½ cups sugar
1½ cups milk
2 eggs plus 1 egg yolk
3½ ounces unsweetened chocolate
½ cup butter

2 cups cake flour
½ teaspoon salt
1½ teaspoons baking soda
1 tablespoon hot water
1 teaspoon vanilla

Combine ½ cup of the sugar, ½ cup of the milk, the egg yolk and the chocolate in a double boiler. Cook and stir until the mixture is smooth and slightly thickened. Remove from heat and cool. Cream the butter with the remaining 1 cup sugar until light and fluffy. Beat the eggs well and combine with the butter and sugar mixture. Sift the flour with the salt and add alternately with the remaining milk. Dissolve the baking soda in the hot water, add to the batter and flavor with vanilla. Blend in the cooled chocolate mixture and pour into 2 9-inch layer cake pans lined with waxed paper (greasing is optional). Bake at 350° F. for 30 minutes. Cool on racks for 5 minutes before removing from the pans. Turn out and remove the waxed paper. Cool. Serves 8 to 10.

SEVEN-MINUTE FROSTING

2 egg whites
1½ cups sugar
¼ teaspoon cream of tartar
⅓ cup water
¼ teaspoon cinnamon

Pinch of salt
1 tablespoon instant coffee (optional)
1 teaspoon vanilla
¾ cup pecans or walnuts (optional)

Put the egg whites, sugar, cream of tartar, water, cinnamon and salt in a double boiler. Add the coffee, if you wish. Cook over moderate heat, beating constantly with a hand or electric beater until the mixture forms peaks. This takes about 7 minutes. Remove from heat and add the vanilla. Beat until the frosting is of spreading consistency. Frost the layers and press nuts around the edge of the cake, if you wish. Yield: Frosting for a 9-inch 2-layer cake.

CHOCOLATE CURLS

1 ounce unsweetened chocolate

Let the chocolate become slightly warmer than room temperature. Cut with a vegetable scraper into curls. Chill before sprinkling on top of frosting as a garnish.

SEMI-BUFFET

Pasta Carbonara
Brochette of Shrimp
Chicken Cacciatora
Baked Spinach
Grapefruit and Avocado Salad
Mocha Ice Cream Pie

PASTA CARBONARA

1½ pounds pasta shells or cappelletti
½ pound lean bacon, cut up
1 medium clove garlic, crushed,
    minced, or diced
4 eggs

¾ cup grated Parmesan cheese
¼ cup minced parsley
½ teaspoon crumbled marjoram or
    oregano (optional)
Dash of hot pepper sauce

Cook pasta in salted water just until *al dente*, about 8 minutes. Meanwhile, sauté bacon until barely crisp, cut up, and add garlic and set aside. Beat eggs with remaining ingredients until thoroughly blended. Add to well drained *hot* pasta, tossing well. Pour on *hot* bacon mixture and toss.

BROCHETTE OF SHRIMP

48 large shrimp
12 tomatoes, quartered

4 slices bacon
Olive oil

Cook the shrimp in a little water until they turn pink, 2 to 3 minutes. Cool and peel. Alternate the shrimp on 8 skewers with tomato wedges and small squares of bacon. Broil only until heated and bacon is crisp, turning once. Brush with olive oil on both sides. Good with rice.

CHICKEN CACCIATORA

2 3-pound chickens
1 teaspoon salt
¼ teaspoon pepper
Flour
3 tablespoons olive oil
2 medium-sized onions, chopped fine
1 clove garlic, crushed

1½ cups tomatoes
1 cup dry white wine
2 tablespoons tomato paste
½ teaspoon oregano
½ teaspoon sugar
½ pound mushrooms, sliced thin

Cut the chickens into serving-sized pieces. Sprinkle with salt, pepper and a little flour and brown in the oil. Add the onion and garlic and brown for about 5 minutes. Add the tomatoes and their juice and the wine mixed with tomato paste. Season with oregano and sugar, cover and simmer for 30 minutes. Add the mushrooms and simmer, uncovered, for 10 minutes. Adjust the seasoning. Often served with spaghetti.

BAKED SPINACH

3 pounds fresh spinach or 3
    10-ounce packages frozen chopped
¾ cup half-and-half
1 teaspoon salt
¼ teaspoon pepper

½ pound mushrooms
¼ cup butter
1 cup bread crumbs
¼ cup grated Parmesan cheese

Wash the spinach and steam in only the water that sticks to the leaves. Cook until limp, about 3 minutes, drain and chop fine. If using frozen, cook according to package instructions. Drain and press out the liquid. Combine spinach with half-and-half, salt and pepper. Wipe the mushrooms and slice thin through heads and stems. Sauté in 2 tablespoons of the butter for 2 or 3 minutes, or until lightly browned. Stir into the spinach, adjust seasoning to taste and spoon into a 3-pint casserole. Sauté the crumbs in the remaining butter for 2 minutes, or until lightly browned. Sprinkle over the spinach and top with cheese. Bake at 350° F. for 15 minutes, raise heat to 450° F. and bake for 10 minutes to brown the top.

GRAPEFRUIT AND AVOCADO SALAD

4 avocados
1 tablespoon lemon juice
4 grapefruit, sectioned [save the juice]
1 tablespoon sugar

1 bunch watercress, or 1 cup shredded
    lettuce
½ cup Lemon French Dressing (see
    page 155 for recipe)

Cut the avocados in half lengthwise, peel and slice. Dip in lemon and grapefruit juice to prevent darkening. Place alternate sections of grapefruit and sliced avocado, petal fashion, on the watercress or shredded lettuce. Serve with the dressing to which you have added the sugar. Serves 8 to 12.

MOCHA ICE CREAM PIE

3 pints coffee ice cream, slightly
  softened
½ cup shaved milk chocolate
1 (9-inch) graham cracker pie shell,
  frozen

Whipped cream (optional)
Chopped nuts (optional)

Thaw ice cream until creamy. Fold in chocolate shavings and pile into pie shell. (See page 157 for recipe.) Freeze until firm. Let stand in refrigerator for about 15 minutes before serving. Top with dollop of whipped cream and nuts, if you wish.

SEMI-BUFFET

Corn on the Cob (when in season)

or

Corn in Butter

or

Corn Pudding

Crown Roast of Pork

Green Mashed Potatoes

Spiced Crab Apples

Peas with Mint and Orange Peel

Spinach, Bean Sprout Salad

Angel Food Cake with Mackenzie Strawberry Frosting

CORN IN BUTTER

8 ears corn (very fresh, please)
¼ cup butter
1 teaspoon salt
½ teaspoon pepper
½ teaspoon sugar (optional)

Cut the corn from the cob, scraping the cob to get juices. Sauté, in butter, cooking only until the butter comes to a full boil. Season with salt, pepper and the sugar, if you wish.

CORN PUDDING

3 cups fresh corn or whole-kernel canned or frozen
½ cup minced scallions
2 tablespoons butter
2 tablespoons flour
2 cups milk
4 eggs, slightly beaten
1 teaspoon salt
¼ teaspoon pepper
2 teaspoons sugar

If using canned corn, drain; if frozen, thaw. Sauté the scallions in butter over low heat for 2 minutes and sprinkle with the flour. Combine the milk and eggs with the salt, pepper and sugar and stir slowly into the onion. Cook, and stir until slightly thickened. Add the corn. Pour into a 2-quart casserole. Bake at 325° F. for about 45 minutes, or until the center is set. Serves 10 to 12.

CROWN ROAST OF PORK

Crown roast of pork
2 teaspoons salt

¼ teaspoon pepper

Have the butcher make the crown. Wipe with a damp cloth and season inside and out with salt and pepper. Place on a rack in an open roaster and roast at 325° F. for 30 to 35 minutes to the pound. Cover the tips of the chops with foil to prevent their burning. It is not necessary to fill the center, but you can fill it with Green Mashed Potatoes (for recipe, see below), and brown with the roast for 30 minutes. Remove the foil and garnish the bones with spiced crab apples or paper frills. Or, fill the center with watercress with the leaves heading up. This is especially nice for the Christmas season if you put red crab apples on the tips of the bones. Count on 1 thick chop per person. Serves 8 to 12.

GREEN MASHED POTATOES

1 recipe Mashed Potatoes (see page 73)
½ cup shredded spinach

¼ cup minced parsley
¼ cup water
Food coloring (optional)

Use the Mashed Potatoes recipe or make them out of instant mashed potatoes, following package instructions for 8 people. Put into a bowl and set aside. Simmer the spinach and parsley in water for a few minutes and force through a sieve or puree in a blender. Stir into the potatoes. If you want a really green look, add a few drops of food coloring. Season to taste.

PEAS WITH MINT AND ORANGE PEEL

4 pounds fresh peas, or 3 10-ounce packages frozen
1 teaspoon salt
3 tablespoons slivered orange peel

½ cup butter
¼ cup finely chopped fresh mint, or 1 teaspoon dried
⅛ teaspoon pepper

Wash, then shell the peas. Put about an inch of water in a large saucepan with the salt and bring to a boil. Add the peas, cover and simmer until tender. If using frozen peas, cook according to package instructions. Heat the orange rind with the butter and let stand a few minutes to steep. When the peas are tender, drain and add the butter and orange peel with the mint. Season with pepper and salt to taste.

SPINACH, BEAN SPROUT SALAD WITH SUNFLOWER SEEDS

2 cups fresh mung bean sprouts or 1
    16-ounce can
1 pound spinach
⅓ cup oil
¼ cup vinegar

2 tablespoons catsup or chili sauce
1 teaspoon salt
¼ teaspoon pepper
½ teaspoon dried rosemary
¼ cup sunflower seeds

Place the sprouts in boiling water for 1 minute and drain. Wash the spinach and tear into bite-sized pieces, removing any tough stems. Combine the spinach and sprouts in a bowl. Mix the remaining ingredients and pour over the salad. Toss and chill.

ANGEL FOOD CAKE

Can be made easily with a mix following package instructions. It is very satisfactory and much less trouble than making one from scratch. Especially good with Mackenzie Strawberry Frosting (see below for recipe). You may fill the inside with fresh berries if you wish.

MACKENZIE STRAWBERRY FROSTING

1 egg white
1 cup sugar

1 cup sliced fresh strawberries

Combine the ingredients in a blender and whirl until thick and fluffy. Yield: frosting for an angel food cake.

SEMI-BUFFET

Easy Lobster Bisque
Roast Loin of Pork
Chicken Tetrazzini
Apple-Horseradish Sauce
Green Beans Succotash
Green Peas
Mixed Green Salad
Fruit Platter
Pecan Cookies

EASY LOBSTER BISQUE

6 ounces lobster meat, or 1 5-ounce can
1 10-ounce can cream of mushroom soup
1 10-ounce can shrimp soup or bisque
2 cups clam broth
2 cups half-and-half
⅓ cup sherry

Shred the lobster or cut into julienne pieces. Combine with the remaining ingredients except the sherry. Heat, without boiling, for 10 minutes. Add the sherry and reheat.

ROAST LOIN OF PORK

(color plate 2)

1 7- to 8-pound loin of pork
¾ cup flour
1¾ teaspoons ground cloves
1 teaspoon salt
1 teaspoon poultry seasoning
½ teaspoon paprika
¼ teaspoon cinnamon
1 cup milk
¼ teaspoon pepper

Have your butcher cut the roast almost all the way through along the bone to facilitate carving. Sift together ½ cup of the flour, cloves, salt, poultry seasoning, paprika and cinnamon. Rub this mixture well into the surface of the roast. Put the pork on a rack in

34

a large roaster and roast, uncovered, for 10 minutes at 500° F. Reduce temperature to 350° F., add about 1 cup of water, cover and roast about 2 hours, or until tender. When done, remove to a hot platter. Skim excess fat from the drippings. Heat the remaining ¼ cup flour in a skillet until slightly tan, add the drippings and gradually the milk. Cook, stirring constantly, until thickened and smooth. Season to taste with salt and the pepper. Serve the gravy on the side. Serves 12.

CHICKEN TETRAZZINI

1 pound spaghetti or spaghettini	1 clove garlic, crushed
2 cups chicken broth, or water with	¼ cup flour
chicken bouillon cubes	½ cup heavy cream
2 cups water	4 cups diced cooked chicken
1½ pounds mushrooms, sliced	½ cup grated Parmesan cheese
¼ cup butter	

Cook the pasta in half water and half chicken broth to cover until barely tender. Drain, reserving the broth. Sauté the mushrooms in 2 tablespoons of the butter with the garlic. Remove and set aside. Add the remaining 2 tablespoons butter and blend in the flour. Gradually stir in 3 cups liquid the spaghetti was cooked in and then the cream. Cook and stir until smooth and thickened. Put a layer of spaghetti in the bottom of a large casserole, cover with chicken and a layer of mushrooms, and add a third of the cream sauce. Sprinkle with Parmesan cheese. Repeat twice, ending with cream sauce and topped with cheese. Bake at 450° F. until bubbling and browned on top, about 20 minutes.

APPLE-HORSERADISH SAUCE

2 cups not-too-sweet applesauce	2 to 4 tablespoons prepared
	horseradish

If you make applesauce don't put too much sugar in it or buy unsweetened and add a little sugar. It is not a dessert. Mix the applesauce with 2 tablespoons of the horseradish. Add more horseradish to taste. Especially good with pork. Yield: 2¼ cups.

GREEN BEANS SUCCOTASH

2 10-ounce packages French-cut green	¼ teaspoon pepper
beans	½ to 1 cup half-and-half
2 10-ounce packages frozen cut corn	Salt to taste
2 tablespoons butter	

Cook the frozen vegetables according to package instructions, being careful not to over-cook. Combine butter, pepper and half-and-half. Taste before adding salt. Add more half-and-half, if you wish. Reheat vegetables and sauce together.

GREEN PEAS

4-5 cups shelled peas	4 scallions, slivered
¼ head either soft lettuce (Boston, Bibb, Leaf, Garden, Escarole, Chicory) or Iceberg	1 teaspoon sugar
	1 teaspoon salt
	⅓ cup melted butter

Put the peas in a pot with the remaining ingredients, except the butter. Do not add moisture as the lettuce will supply enough. Steam for 15 minutes. Serve with melted butter. If using frozen peas, you will need 3 10-ounce packages, thawed. Cook with lettuce using no water for 10 minutes.

MIXED GREEN SALAD

1 head Romaine	3 tablespoons minced chives or scallions
1 head chicory or escarole	⅓ cup minced parsley
1 bunch leaf lettuce	½ cup French Dressing (see page 155 for recipe)

Pull apart, wash and dry the greens. Break into bite-sized pieces. Put into a bowl with the chives or scallions and parsley and toss. Chill until serving time. Pour the dressing over and toss thoroughly. Serves 12.

FRUIT PLATTER

Count on ¾ to 1 cup of fruit per person. Vary the combinations according to colors and textures and the availability at market. The various fruit should be in separate piles with a bowl or scooped out half melon in the center with whipped cream, ice cream, sherbet or fine sugar. Each person takes what he likes best from a choice of four to six kinds: strawberries, blackberries, blueberries, raspberries, sliced peaches, nectarines or apricots, pitted cherries, seedless grapes, sliced or shredded pineapple, sliced bananas, cantaloupe, honeydew, watermelon or other melon balls. Sugar the berries and peaches slightly. Cut bananas at the last minute. Chill bowl (chill or freeze the scooped out melon) if it's to hold ice cream or sherbet. This is a spectacular buffet dessert.

PECAN COOKIES

1 cup brown sugar	1 egg white, beaten stiff
1 tablespoon flour	1 cup chopped pecans
⅛ teaspoon salt	

Mix the brown sugar, flour and salt. Carefully fold in the egg white. Fold in the pecans. Drop by teaspoonfuls onto a greased baking sheet. Bake at 300° F. for 15 minutes. Let cool a little before removing from the baking sheet. Yield: 2 dozen.

SEMI-BUFFET

Pea Soup
Boned Rib Roast (Eye of the Prime)
Cheese-Stuffed Potatoes
Cauliflower Puree
Green Beans
Herbed Tomatoes
Assorted Glazed Fruit Tarts

PEA SOUP

1½ pounds split green peas, unsoaked (almost 3 cups)
10 cups water
2 smoked ham hocks (about 1½ pounds)
2½ cups peeled, diced potatoes

¾ cup diced carrots
¾ cup chopped celery with some leaves
2 leeks (white part only), sliced thin
1 cup chopped onion
1 teaspoon salt

In large heavy pot bring peas and water to boil, reduce heat and simmer for 2 minutes. Remove from heat, cover and let stand for 1 hour. Add ham hocks, bring to boil, reduce heat, cover and simmer for 1 hour. Add vegetables and simmer, covered, for 2 hours. Remove ham hocks and let cool slightly. Trim off fat and discard. Cut meat from bone, slice and return to soup. Add salt. If soup seems too thick, thin with hot water or chicken bouillon.

BONED RIB ROAST

(Eye of the Prime)

1 5- to 6-pound rib roast, boned and tied
2 teaspoons salt
¼ teaspoon pepper

1 cup chopped onion
½ cup water
Steak sauce (optional)
Red wine (optional)

Put the roast in an open roasting pan. Season with salt and pepper and add the onion. Roast at 350° F. for about 20 minutes to the pound (125° on a meat thermometer for rare and it should be rare). Remove meat to a hot platter. If you want gravy, add the water, steak sauce and, if you wish, a little red wine to the drippings. Bring to a boil over direct heat and skim off the fat. Reseason to taste. Serve the juices on the side or pour over the meat. Serves 12.

CHEESE-STUFFED POTATOES

8 large potatoes baked, and flesh
   scooped out of skins
½ cup cream, heated
2 tablespoons butter

4 tablespoons grated cheese
1 teaspoon salt
⅛ teaspoon pepper

Whip the potatoes with the cream and butter. Add 2 tablespoons of the cheese, salt and pepper. When fluffy, refill the potato skins and sprinkle the remaining 2 tablespoons cheese on top. Reheat in a 400° F. oven for 5 to 7 minutes, or until the cheese melts.

CAULIFLOWER PUREE

1 very large or 2 small heads
   cauliflower
1 teaspoon salt
¼ teaspoon white pepper

3 tablespoons instant mashed
   potatoes cooked in milk
Butter (optional)

Steam the cauliflower with the salt and pepper on a rack for 20 minutes, or until soft. Cool slightly and break into pieces. Puree in a food processor or blender. Mix with the mashed potatoes, adjust the seasoning and reheat for 2 minutes. Add butter, if you wish.

GREEN BEANS

1½ pounds young green beans, ends
   trimmed

3 tablespoons butter

Arrange beans in bundles and tie with string. Drop into lightly salted boiling water, cover and simmer for 10 minutes, or until crisp-tender. Drain well in colander. Melt butter in same pot, add the beans and turn to coat. They are more attractive on the buffet if they are arranged in one direction.

HERBED TOMATOES

6 large or 9 medium-sized tomatoes, peeled and sliced
3 tablespoons olive oil
1 teaspoon salt
1 teaspoon sugar
2 tablespoons minced chives or scallions

1 tablespoon fresh basil, or 1 teaspoon dried
1 tablespoon fresh thyme, or 1 teaspoon dried
1 tablespoon fresh oregano, or ½ teaspoon dried
2 tablespoons minced parsley

Put the tomatoes, slices overlapping slightly, on a platter or shallow bowl. Combine the remaining ingredients except the parsley. Shake thoroughly and pour over the tomatoes. Chill for 3 or 4 hours or longer. Serve garnished with parsley. Serves 10 to 12.

ASSORTED GLAZED FRUIT TARTS

(color plate 7)

1 envelope gelatin
2 tablespoons sugar
¼ cup water
1½ cups orange juice
1 teaspoon orange extract or grated orange peel

8 commercial dessert shells
¼ cup each: blueberries, seedless grapes, halved pitted cherries, sliced small plums, apricots, nectarines, peaches, kiwi fruits or strawberries

In small saucepan combine gelatin, sugar and water. Stir over low heat until gelatin dissolves. Remove from heat and stir in orange juice and extract. Chill until consistency of unbeaten egg whites. Meanwhile place dessert shells on rack in jelly roll pan. Fill cavities with fruit. Spoon orange glaze over fruit and shells, respooning any that runs into pan. Chill until set.

SEMI-BUFFET

Vegetarian

Garden Vegetable Soup
Brown Rice Salad with Vegetables
Zucchini with Parmesan Cheese
Crookneck Squash
Tomato and Alfalfa Sprout Salad
Mushroom Salad
Baked Macaroni and Cheese
Easy Grape Dessert
Lace Cookies

GARDEN VEGETABLE SOUP

(color plate 4)

½ cup chopped celery
½ cup chopped onion
2 tablespoons oil
4 cups chicken broth
4 large tomatoes, peeled and chopped
½ pound green beans, cut into ½-inch pieces
1 large carrot, sliced
1 tablespoon chopped fresh basil, or 1 teaspoon dried
1 teaspoon sugar
1 bay leaf, crumbled
2 small zucchini, sliced thin
1 cup corn, cut off cob
1 teaspoon salt
½ teaspoon pepper

In large saucepan sauté celery and onion in oil until tender. Add broth, tomatoes, beans, carrot, basil, sugar and bay leaf. Bring to boil, reduce heat, cover and simmer for 30 minutes. Add zucchini and corn, return to boil and simmer covered for 5 minutes, or until tender. Season with salt and pepper.

BROWN RICE SALAD WITH VEGETABLES

2 cups brown rice
2 teaspoons oil
3 cups water
½ cup broth
1 teaspoon salt
½ cup shredded celery
½ cup shredded carrot

½ cup shredded zucchini or seeded
   cucumber
2 tablespoons minced onion
1 small green pepper, slivered
2 tablespoons chopped parsley
1 teaspoon lemon juice
¾ cup French Dressing (see page 155
   for recipe)

Sauté the rice in the oil for 3 minutes, then add the water, broth and salt. Cover and simmer for about 20 minutes, or until tender. Cool. Toss with the vegetables. Add lemon juice to the dressing, pour over the salad and toss. Chill.

ZUCCHINI WITH PARMESAN CHEESE

6 to 8 small zucchini
1 teaspoon salt
3 tablespoons melted butter

3 tablespoons grated Parmesan cheese
3 tablespoons minced parsley

Scrape the zucchini, leaving most of the skin on. Place on the rack of a steamer, sprinkle with salt and butter and steam for about 10 minutes. Or, wrap in foil and steam in a 400° F. oven for 15 to 20 minutes, if you like. To serve, transfer to a warm platter or vegetable dish and sprinkle with the cheese and parsley.

CROOKNECK SQUASH

8 small yellow crookneck, whole and
   unpeeled
2 tablespoons melted butter
1 tablespoon olive oil

1 teaspoon salt
1 tablespoon minced chives
1 teaspoon sage

Steam the squash in butter for 15 minutes. Add the remaining ingredients. Serve hot. Zucchini, summer or crookneck squash may be sautéed in 3 tablespoons butter for 3 or 4 minutes and seasoned with salt, pepper and one of the suggested herbs. This is done quickly, cooking no more than 3 or 4 minutes.

TOMATO AND ALFALFA SPROUT SALAD

6 large ripe tomatoes, peeled
1 teaspoon sugar
1½ teaspoons salt
¼ cup oil
1 cup alfalfa sprouts

¼ cup chopped scallions
1 tablespoon fresh basil, chopped, or 1
   teaspoon dried
1 teaspoon lemon juice
1 tablespoon minced parsley (garnish)

Slice the tomatoes and place them, slightly overlapping, on a platter. Sprinkle with the sugar and 1 teaspoon of the salt. Pour over half of the oil. Cover with the sprouts mixed with scallions and basil. Add the lemon juice to the remaining oil and remaining ½ teaspoon salt, and pour over the tomatoes. Sprinkle with parsley and chill.

MUSHROOM SALAD

3 pounds small mushrooms
3 white onions, sliced thin

⅓ cup Lemon French Dressing (see page 155 for recipe)
2 tablespoons minced fresh tarragon or oregano, or 2 teaspoons dried

Wipe the mushrooms with a damp towel. You may have to cut the ends if they are sandy. Slice thin through the cap and stem. Combine the mushrooms, onion and herbs and toss with the dressing. Chill for several hours. Serves 10 to 12.

BAKED MACARONI AND CHEESE

1½ pounds elbow macaroni
¼ cup butter
¼ cup flour
3 cups milk

¾ pound Cheddar cheese, shredded or grated
½ cup bread crumbs
½ cup grated Parmesan cheese

Cook the macaroni according to package instructions. Melt the butter, blend in the flour and stir in the milk gradually. Add the Cheddar cheese and cook, stirring, until smooth and thickened. Put the drained macaroni into a buttered large shallow casserole or square Pyrex dish (everyone likes the top crust). Pour the cheese sauce over. Top with bread crumbs or Parmesan cheese or with a mixture of the two. Bake at 350° F. for about 30 minutes, or until bubbly and browned on top.

EASY GRAPE DESSERT

2½ to 3 pounds seedless grapes
1½ cups sour cream

¾ cup brown sugar (either light or dark)

Pull the grapes from their stems, wash and dry them. Mix the sour cream with the brown sugar. Put the grapes into the cream mixture and stir well. Chill for several hours.

LACE COOKIES

½ cup sugar
½ cup flour
Pinch of salt
¼ teaspoon baking powder
½ cup old-fashioned oats

2 tablespoons cream
2 tablespoons light corn syrup
⅓ cup melted butter
1 tablespoon vanilla

Sift the sugar, flour, salt and baking powder into a bowl. Add the remaining ingredients and mix together until well blended. Using a ¼-teaspoon measuring spoon, drop about 4 inches apart onto an ungreased baking sheet. Bake at 375° F. for 6 to 8 minutes, or until lightly browned. Let cool a few seconds before removing from the baking sheet. Yield: 6 dozen 2-inch cookies.

SEMI-BUFFET

Vegetarian

Egg-Spinach Soup
Black Bean Enchiladas
Mushrooms on Whole-Wheat Toast
Basic Stuffed Tomatoes
Cucumber Salad
Tofu Vegetable Salad
Carrot Cake

EGG-SPINACH SOUP WITH CHEESE

6 cups beef broth
2 pounds fresh spinach, tough stems discarded and leaves torn into small pieces
4 eggs

½ cup grated Parmesan cheese
½ teaspoon salt
¼ teaspoon pepper

In a Dutch oven bring broth to boil. Add spinach, cover and simmer for 5 minutes or until spinach is tender. Meanwhile, beat eggs with 2 tablespoons of the cheese until well blended. While stirring, pour egg mixture in steady thin stream into simmering soup. Simmer for 1 minute, or until eggs are cooked. Season with salt and pepper. Serve topped with remaining cheese.

BLACK BEAN ENCHILADAS

1 cup minced onion
2 cloves garlic, minced
6 tablespoons oil
1 16-ounce can black beans
2 tablespoons chopped cilantro or
  parsley
2 teaspoons cumin
2 teaspoons chili powder

1 teaspoon salt
1 10-ounce can mild enchilada sauce
16 large corn tortillas
6 ounces shredded medium or sharp
  Cheddar cheese
½ cup chopped walnuts
Chopped cilantro for garnish
  (optional)

In a medium saucepan sauté ½ cup of the onion and the garlic in 2 tablespoons oil until onion is tender. Stir in beans, cilantro or parsley, cumin, chili powder and salt, mixing well. Then remove from heat. In large skillet over medium heat in 3 tablespoons each oil and enchilada sauce heat tortillas a few at a time on both sides, just until soft and saturated. Place on paper towels, continuing until all tortillas are heated, adding more oil and sauce as needed. To assemble enchiladas, reserve ½ cup cheese. Spread a heaping tablespoon black bean mixture over each tortilla, sprinkle with layer of cheese, roll up and place, seam side down, in greased shallow baking dish. Pour remaining enchilada sauce evenly over filled enchiladas. Sprinkle with reserved cheese and walnuts. Cover dish tight with foil, bake at 350° F. for 20 minutes, or until cheese is bubbling. Remove foil and sprinkle with chopped cilantro. To serve, use 2 spatulas to prevent enchiladas from falling apart.

MUSHROOMS ON WHOLE-WHEAT TOAST

2 pounds mushrooms
½ cup chopped onion
¼ cup butter
1 teaspoon oregano or thyme
1 teaspoon salt

¼ teaspoon pepper
2 tablespoons Worcestershire sauce
2 tablespoons flour
1 cup cream or half-and-half

Wipe the mushrooms and unless they are small, cut in halves. Sauté the onion in butter for 2 minutes. Add the mushrooms, oregano or thyme, salt and pepper. Cook and stir for 2 minutes. Add the Worcestershire sauce, turn off the heat, cover and let stand for a few minutes. This can be done ahead of time. Sprinkle with flour, stir and reheat. Pour in the cream slowly and let come to a boil, stirring gently. Serve on whole-wheat toast.

BASIC STUFFED TOMATOES

10 medium-sized, ripe tomatoes
Salt
½ teaspoon sugar
½ cup chopped scallions or minced
  onion

¾ cup chopped celery
½ cup Mayonnaise (see page 154 for
  recipe)

Cut the tops off tomatoes and scoop out the flesh and seeds, leaving about ¼-inch in the shells. Chop the tomato pulp and reserve. Salt the inside of the tomato shells slightly and turn them upside down to drain. Chill them while you make the filling. Drain the tomato pulp and add it along with the sugar, scallions or onion and celery to the mayonnaise. Toss. If this mixture is too thick, add a little of the juice from the tomatoes. Fill the chilled tomato shells, piling up the filling to give a generous look. Chill several hours before serving.

CUCUMBER SALAD

4 large or 6 small cucumbers	1 tablespoon sugar
1 large sweet onion, sliced thin	⅓ cup French Dressing (see page 155
½ teaspoon salt	for recipe)
¼ teaspoon pepper	Vinegar (optional)
	Minced chives, parsley or fresh dill

Peel the cucumbers and scrape from top to bottom with the tines of a fork. Slice as thin as possible (a processor is excellent for slicing). Layer into a salad bowl with the onion. Combine the salt, pepper and sugar with the dressing, adding a little extra vinegar to taste; you want a tart dressing. Pour the dressing over and toss. Add the chives, parsley or dill and toss again. If the cucumbers seem too wet, pour off excess dressing before serving.

TOFU VEGETABLE SALAD

½ cup plain yogurt	1 small cucumber, peeled and sliced
¼ cup minced cilantro or parsley	thin
(cilantro is Italian or Chinese	2 large tomatoes, cubed
parsley)	1 cup sliced mushrooms
3 tablespoons lemon juice	6 scallions, sliced
¼ teaspoon ginger	2 medium-sized oranges, peeled and
1 teaspoon salt	sectioned
¼ teaspoon pepper	2 small bananas, sliced
1 pound firm-style tofu, cut into	½ cup chopped walnuts
½-inch cubes	Shredded cilantro or parsley for
2 cloves garlic, minced	garnish (optional)
3 tablespoons oil	Shredded lettuce

In small bowl mix well yogurt, cilantro or parsley, lemon juice, ginger, salt and pepper. Chill. In small skillet sauté tofu and garlic in oil for 5 minutes, or until tofu is lightly browned. Remove and drain on paper towels. In large bowl gently toss tofu with remaining ingredients except lettuce and cilantro leaves. Add chilled dressing, tossing gently. Chill for at least 2 hours. Spoon onto lettuce and garnish with cilantro.

CARROT CAKE

1½ cups flour
1¼ cups sugar
1½ teaspoons baking soda
1½ teaspoons cinnamon
¼ teaspoon salt
2 4½-ounce jars strained carrots
⅔ cup oil

2 eggs, slightly beaten
½ teaspoon vanilla
1 8-ounce can crushed pineapple, drained
⅔ cup coconut
½ cup chopped walnuts
Cream Cheese Frosting (recipe follows)

In a 9-inch square pan with fork mix well flour, sugar, baking soda, cinnamon and salt. Add carrots, oil, eggs and vanilla. Mix briskly with fork until thoroughly blended. Stir in pineapple, coconut and walnuts. Bake at 350° F. for 40 to 45 minutes, or until a pick inserted in center comes out clean and cake pulls away from sides of pan. Place the pan on a rack to cool. Spread with frosting.

CREAM CHEESE FROSTING

1 3-ounce package cream cheese, softened
¼ cup butter, softened

½ teaspoon vanilla
2 cups confectioners' sugar

With wooden spoon, mix cream cheese, butter and vanilla until well blended. Add sugar and beat until smooth. Frost cake.

II

HOT BUFFETS

If the guests can sit at a table to eat, you may serve practically anything on a buffet that you would serve at a formal dinner. If you wish to start with soup, it can be served in mugs. Food placed on a hot tray will stay at the proper temperature; modern oven-to-table ware maintains its heat for a long time; chafing dishes are also useful. These menus are planned with this in mind and are also designed so that a great deal of the preparation and cooking can be done ahead of time. The dishes have been carefully selected so that nothing requires last-minute attention or has to be eaten promptly, like a soufflé.

Certain meals are actually more appropriate on a buffet than at a dining table. With curry, for example, the many condiments add dramatic appeal and permit each person to take what he wants. A vegetable platter may offer three or four vegetables, so at least one or two will (with luck!) appeal to everyone. You may decide to serve two entrées, which would not be done at a formal dinner, since, unless there was a menu on the table, no one would expect a second main dish. This, of course, is not a problem when the guests can see exactly what there is for dinner.

HOT BUFFET

Prosciutto and Lettuce Salad
Roast Lamb Chops
Couscous
Green Beans with Almonds
Lima Beans
Apple and Beet Salad
Lemon Angel Pie

PROSCIUTTO AND LETTUCE SALAD

(color plate 1)

2 tablespoons red wine vinegar
½ teaspoon salt
¼ teaspoon freshly ground pepper
⅓ cup olive oil
16 very thin slices prosciutto

12 cups loosely packed, torn leaf
lettuce
¾ cup lightly toasted chopped
walnuts
3 tablespoons grated Parmesan cheese

To make dressing, stir together vinegar, salt and pepper. Beat in oil until well blended. Toss lettuce with enough dressing to coat and arrange on platter. Toss nuts with dressing, sprinkle over lettuce. Sprinkle with Parmesan. Drape prosciutto over the lettuce.

ROAST LAMB CHOPS

8 (2-inch) loin lamb chops
8 slices bacon
1 teaspoon salt

½ teaspoon pepper
¼ teaspoon rosemary
Flour

Fold the tail of each chop to make a circle and wind the bacon around. Fasten the bacon with a toothpick. Sprinkle with salt, pepper and rosemary and dredge lightly with flour. Place in a roasting pan and brown on both sides under the broiler. Transfer to a 400° F. oven, add a little water to the pan and bake for 15 minutes. Obviously, these are easy to serve on a buffet.

COUSCOUS

1 (1 pound) package couscous
4 cups broth or part water
½ teaspoon salt

¼ cup butter
Salt (optional)

Moisten the couscous slowly with a little water, mixing it, preferably with your fingers, until wet and smooth. There must be no lumps. Set it aside for 30 minutes. Put the couscous in a pot with the broth and salt and simmer or steam until tender, about 15 minutes. Add butter. If you have used mostly water instead of broth, you will need more salt.

GREEN BEANS WITH ALMONDS

1½ pounds green beans
1 cup water
1 teaspoon salt

¼ teaspoon pepper
½ cup slivered almonds
¼ cup butter

Trim and cut the beans French-style, unless they are small and young, in which case leave them whole. Boil in water for 10 to 12 minutes until crisp-tender. Drain and add salt and pepper. Meanwhile, sauté the almonds in butter for 2 or 3 minutes until light brown. Stir the almonds and the butter with the beans and reheat.

LIMA BEANS

3 pounds fresh small lima beans or 3
   10-ounce packages frozen
¼ cup butter
¼ teaspoon pepper

¼ teaspoon nutmeg
2 tablespoons minced parsley or
   chives
Salt (optional)

Cook the beans in salted water for 10 to 15 minutes, or until tender. If using frozen, cook according to package instructions. Drain. Toss with the remaining ingredients. You may need to add a little salt.

APPLE AND BEET SALAD

3 medium-sized apples, peeled and
   diced
2 cups diced, pickled beets
⅓ cup pickle relish
¼ cup minced onion
¼ cup Mayonnaise (see page 154 for
   recipe)

1 tablespoon sugar
2 tablespoons cider vinegar
¼ teaspoon salt
⅛ teaspoon pepper
Lettuce leaves
1 hard-cooked egg, chopped

In mixing bowl gently mix well all ingredients except lettuce and egg. Spoon into a lettuce-lined serving dish and garnish top with egg.

LEMON ANGEL PIE

Crust:

3 egg whites
Pinch of salt
¼ teaspoon cream of tartar

1 teaspoon lemon juice
¾ cup superfine sugar
1 teaspoon vanilla

Filling:

6 egg yolks
¾ cup sugar
⅓ cup lemon juice

1½ tablespoons grated lemon peel
1 cup heavy cream

Crust:

Beat the egg whites with the salt until the whites are frothy. Add the cream of tartar and lemon juice, and continue to beat until the whites form soft peaks when the beater is lifted. Gradually add the superfine sugar while continuing to beat. When the meringue is thick and glossy, stir in the vanilla. Spread the meringue thickly over the bottom and sides of a well buttered 9-inch pie plate. Bake the meringue in a 250° F. oven for 30 to 45 minutes, or until it is dry. Loosen it from the pan while it is still warm and allow to cool on a cake rack.

Filling:

In the top of a double boiler, beat the egg yolks until they are thick and lemon colored. Gradually beat in the sugar. Add the lemon juice and peel. Cook over simmering water, stirring constantly, until it is thick. Remove from the heat and cool thoroughly.

Spread the filling in the shell and top it with the heavy cream that has been whipped until it is thick and glossy. Chill the pie overnight.

HOT BUFFET

California (Caesar) Salad
Fish Stew with Mushrooms
Roast Fillet of Beef
Stuffed Potatoes with Sour Cream
Three Vegetable Platter
(Carrots, Broccoli and Cauliflower)
Chocolate Mousse
Ladyfingers

CALIFORNIA (CAESAR) SALAD

1 large head lettuce
1 head romaine
1 egg, coddled for 1 minute
6 to 8 anchovies, chopped
½ teaspoon freshly ground pepper

1 tablespoon Worcestershire sauce
¼ cup grated Parmesan cheese
½ cup Lemon French Dressing (see page 155 for recipe)
2 cups garlic croutons

Wash the greens and dry thoroughly. Break up into a large bowl. Open the egg into a bowl and add the remaining ingredients, except croutons. Mix thoroughly and pour over the greens. Add the croutons and toss.

FISH STEW WITH MUSHROOMS

3 to 3½ pounds fish fillets
2 medium-sized onions, chopped
2 tablespoons butter
3 tablespoons flour
4 cups fish or chicken broth, or a combination

¼ cup tomato puree
1 pound mushrooms, sliced
2 dill pickles, chopped (optional)
2 tablespoons fresh dill or 2 teaspoons dried
1 tablespoon lemon juice

Cut the fish fillets into bite-sized pieces. Sauté the onion in the butter until light brown. Stir in the flour and then the broth. Add the tomato puree and simmer for 10 minutes. Add the mushrooms, pickles, dill and the fish. Simmer gently for about 10 minutes, or until the fish is done but not falling apart. Add the lemon juice. Serves 8 to 10.

ROAST FILLET OF BEEF

1 4- to 5-pound fillet of beef
1 teaspoon salt

¼ teaspoon pepper
½ cup Burgundy (optional)

Trim the fat from the beef and sprinkle with salt and pepper. Place in a pan on the broiler rack and broil for 20 minutes. Reduce heat to 300° F. and bake in the oven for 20 minutes more, basting with the wine if you wish. The beef should be rare. Place the beef on a platter and pour the drippings over. Carve in slices ½ inch thick, allowing two per person. Count on a little less than ½ pound per person. Serves 8 to 12.

STUFFED POTATOES WITH SOUR CREAM

1 cup sour cream
8 large baked potatoes, flesh scooped
   out
¼ cup chopped chives or scallions

1 teaspoon salt
¼ teaspoon pepper
Butter

Leave the sour cream at room temperature for several hours. Rice or whip the potato flesh until smooth. Mix the cream with the chives, salt and pepper. Stir into the potatoes. Fill the shells lightly with this mixture and heat thoroughly in the oven.

THREE VEGETABLE PLATTER

Serve three vegetables on one large platter. Arrange colors attractively.

Carrots
Broccoli
Cauliflower

CHOCOLATE MOUSSE

6 ounces semisweet or sweet
   chocolate
5 eggs, separated

2 tablespoons very strong coffee and/
   or rum

Melt the chocolate slowly in the top of a double boiler over hot water until smooth. Remove from heat and let cool slightly. Beat the egg yolks slightly and mix with the chocolate. Add the coffee and/or rum. Beat the egg whites until stiff and fold in. Pour into pot de crème cups, demitasses or small custard cups. You may use a china or glass serving dish. Chill for several hours.

You may double or triple this recipe for a large group.

HOT BUFFET

Scallops in Shell (Coquilles St. Jacques)
Cornish Game Hens
Zucchini Cheese Boats
Green Rice Salad
Eggplant with Tomato Slices
Pineapple Filled with Fruit
Loaf Cake

SCALLOPS IN SHELLS

(Coquilles St. Jacques)

2 pounds bay scallops (if not
   available, use sea scallops)
½ cup water
½ cup white wine
8 shallots, minced
3 tablespoons butter
¼ pound mushrooms, sliced thin

½ teaspoon salt
¼ teaspoon pepper
3 tablespoons flour
2 tablespoons minced parsley
   (optional)
Bread crumbs
Grated Swiss or Parmesan cheese

If using sea scallops, cut into 2 to 4 pieces each and simmer 2 minutes; bay scallops, which are small, don't need to be cut. Put the scallops in a sauce pan with the water and white wine almost to cover. Simmer for 3 minutes. Drain, reserving the liquid. Sauté the shallots in the butter for 2 to 3 minutes. Add the mushrooms, salt and pepper and simmer for another 2 or 3 minutes. Stir in the flour and the liquid from the scallops. Cook and stir until thickened. Add the scallops and the parsley, if you wish. Reheat. Divide among 8 shell-shaped dishes. Sprinkle lightly with bread crumbs and cheese. Brown under the broiler or in the oven. NOTE: They are especially easy to serve at a buffet since each person takes a shell.

CORNISH GAME HENS

8 small or 4 large game hens
1 teaspoon salt
½ teaspoon pepper

Rice or Kasha Stuffing (see page 141 for recipe)
½ cup butter, melted
Chicken broth

Large birds are too big for a serving as the entrée of a dinner. If you cannot get small ones, serve only half hens and do not stuff them. Rub the birds with the salt and pepper. Fill with the stuffing of your choice. Fasten skin over with poultry pins or toothpicks, or sew shut. Bake, breast side up, at 450° F. for 20 minutes, reduce heat to 350° F. and bake for 30 minutes longer. Baste several times with a mixture of the butter and chicken broth.

ZUCCHINI CHEESE BOATS

8 small zucchini
1 teaspoon salt
½ teaspoon pepper

¾ cup grated sharp Cheddar cheese
Paprika

Wash the zucchini and slice in half lengthwise. Parboil in salted water until just tender (approximately 2 minutes) in a covered skillet. Don't let the zucchini get mushy. Drain. Scoop out some of the seedy portion in the center of each half. Season the shells with salt and pepper. Fill with the grated cheese and sprinkle with a little paprika. Broil until the cheese melts and serve immediately.

GREEN RICE SALAD

3 cups rice
1 teaspoon salt
5½ cups water
¼ cup vinegar
½ cup oil

½ cup minced parsley
¼ cup minced scallions
¼ cup chopped green pepper
½ cup tightly packed chopped watercress leaves

Cook the rice covered in salted water for 20 minutes or until tender and all water is absorbed. Stir in the vinegar and oil. Cool. Combine the vegetables, stir into the rice and mix well. Chill. Serves 12 to 14.

EGGPLANT WITH TOMATO SLICES

(color plate 4)

4 ½-inch thick slices eggplant
1 large tomato, cut into 4 thick slices
½ small green pepper, cut into 4 chunks

¼ cup butter or margarine
2 tablespoons seasoned bread crumbs
1 hard-cooked egg

In large skillet in a single layer cook eggplant, tomato and green pepper in butter for 3 to 5 minutes on each side, or until browned and tender.

Remove eggplant to serving plate and top each slice with tomato and green pepper. Add bread crumbs to skillet and sauté about 1 minute, or until lightly browned. Sprinkle crumbs on vegetables. Press egg through sieve or mash with fork and sprinkle over crumbs. Serves 4.

PINEAPPLE FILLED WITH FRUIT

| 2 large pineapples | 4 to 5 cups assorted cut-up fruit |

Cut the pineapple in half lengthwise through the leaves. Scrape out the flesh and dice it. You may freeze the shells and fill them when ready to serve. This ensures cold fruit and prevents the juices running out. The assorted fruits may be made up of diced pineapple, berries, melon cubes, sliced peaches, persimmons, bananas and/or pitted cherries. Serves 8 to 10.

LOAF CAKE

2 cups flour	½ cup butter or margarine, softened
1 teaspoon baking soda	1 cup packed light brown sugar
½ teaspoon baking powder	1 egg, at room temperature
½ teaspoon salt	1¼ cups applesauce, at room
1 teaspoon cinnamon	temperature
½ teaspoon nutmeg	½ cup raisins
¼ teaspoon cloves	½ cup chopped walnuts
¼ teaspoon allspice	

Mix well flour, soda, baking powder, salt and spices. Set aside. Cream butter and sugar together. Add egg, and beat until fluffy. Stir in flour mixture and applesauce. Stir in raisins and nuts. Turn into greased and lightly floured 9 x 5 x 3-inch loaf pan. Bake at 350° F. 70 minutes, or until a pick inserted in center comes out clean. Cool in pan on rack 5 minutes. Remove from pan and cool completely. Serve plain or frost as desired.

HOT BUFFET

Blender Gazpacho
Bread Sticks and Assorted Crackers
Duck with Orange
Fish Fillets in Foil
Broccoli with Mushrooms
Cooked Vegetable Salad
Apricot Tart

BLENDER GAZPACHO

6 large tomatoes, peeled and cut up,
    or 2 1-pound cans Italian plum
    tomatoes
1 sweet onion, cut up, or 6 scallions,
    cut up
2 small cucumbers, peeled and cut up
½ green pepper, seeded and chopped
2 cloves garlic, slivered

2 tablespoons bread crumbs
1 teaspoon salt
¼ teaspoon pepper
2 teaspoons sugar
½ teaspoon tarragon
3 tablespoons olive oil
2 tablespoons vinegar
2 cups chicken or beef broth

This is better made with fresh tomatoes, if good ones are available. Put all the ingredients in a large bowl and mix. Ladle into a blender or processor. Serve with ice cubes, which may be put into a tureen at the last minute. Serves 10.

DUCK WITH ORANGE

2 5-pound ducks	5 teaspoons salt
2 cups water	½ teaspoon pepper
1 onion	3 oranges
¼ teaspoon thyme	½ cup white wine
½ bay leaf	Flour-and-water paste

Put the giblets, necks and wing tips in a pot with the water, onion, thyme, bay leaf and 1 teaspoon of the salt. Simmer for 45 minutes. Meanwhile, rub the ducks each with 1 teaspoon of the salt and ¼ teaspoon of the pepper. Cut 1 orange into 8 pieces (rind and all) and put 4 in the cavity of each duck. Roast in a 450° F. oven for 20 minutes. Meanwhile, slice 1 orange very thin. Grate the peel from the remaining orange with a coarse grater to make slivers and then squeeze the juice. Prick the breasts of the ducks to release the fat and pour off excess fat. Reduce oven temperature to 350° F. Pour over the wine, orange juice and remaining 2 teaspoons salt and cook for 1 hour. Baste every 10 minutes, turning the birds to brown evenly. If not brown enough, raise the heat to 450° F. and bake 10 minutes longer. Place the ducks on a platter and keep warm. Skim the fat from the pan juices. Add the orange peel and 1 cup strained broth from the giblets. Thicken with a flour-and-water paste.

FISH FILLETS IN FOIL

8 to 12 fillets of flounder, sole or other fish (about ⅓ pound each)	¼ teaspoon pepper
Soft butter	3 tablespoons wine, wine vinegar, clam broth or lemon juice
1 teaspoon salt	Herbs (optional)

Place each fillet on a piece of buttered foil. Sprinkle with a little salt and pepper and add about 1 teaspoon of the liquid of your choice. You may also sprinkle with an herb if you wish: dill, basil, parsley, thyme, oregano or chives. Bake in a 400° F. oven for about 25 minutes. Serves 8 to 12.

BROCCOLI WITH MUSHROOMS

1 pound mushrooms	4 bunches broccoli, with stems scraped
¼ cup butter	

Cut mushrooms in half, if large, and brown in the butter for 2 minutes. Add to the broccoli which has been steamed. Toss. Serves 10 to 12.

COOKED VEGETABLE SALAD

2 stalks celery, scraped and diced
1 10-ounce package frozen peas
1 10-ounce package small lima beans
1 10-ounce package cut green beans
1 10-ounce package diced carrots

1 12-ounce can diced beets
4 new potatoes, cooked, peeled and diced
¼ to ⅓ cup French Dressing (see page 155 for recipe)

Put the celery in a little salted water and cook about 5 minutes. Drain. Cook the frozen vegetables, following package instructions. You may cook some together in the same pot if the cooking time is about the same. Drain the beets and rinse them under cold running water. Drain and combine all the vegetables in a bowl, adding the potatoes. Mix thoroughly. Pour on the dressing sparingly and toss. Chill. This salad should not be too wet since it goes on the dinner plate with the entrée. Serves 8 to 10.

APRICOT TART

(color plate 7)

1 cup flour
¼ cup ground or finely chopped blanched almonds
2 tablespoons granulated sugar
¼ teaspoon salt
½ cup butter or margarine, slightly softened
1 8-ounce package Neufchâtel cheese, softened

¼ cup confectioners' sugar
½ teaspoon almond extract
1 pound medium-sized apricots, halved (about 8)
2 tablespoons currant jelly (optional)
½ cup apricot preserves
1 tablespoon lemon juice, or to taste

In a medium bowl combine flour, almonds, granulated sugar and salt. Cut in butter or margarine until particles resemble coarse crumbs. Shape into dough and press firmly onto sides and bottom of loose-bottom 9-inch tart pan or springform pan. Chill for 30 minutes. Bake at 425° F. for 10 to 12 minutes, or until golden. Cool on rack, then remove rim of pan. One hour before serving, beat cheese with confectioners' sugar and almond extract until smooth. Spread in cooled tart shell. Arrange apricot halves, pitted side up, on cheese mixture. Fill apricot cavities with currant jelly. Stir to blend apricot preserves with lemon juice. Spoon over apricots.

HOT BUFFET
Chinese food is ideal for a buffet.

Pork-Cucumber Soup
Fried Rice
Pork Chop Suey
Crab-Pork-Pepper Wedges
Sweet and Sour Chicken
Fortune Cookies
Leechi Nuts
Pineapple Chunks (on toothpicks)
Tea

PORK-CUCUMBER SOUP

6 cups chicken broth
3 tablespoons soy sauce
2 scallions, sliced thin
¾ pound lean boneless pork, cut into thin strips

2 cucumbers, peeled, halved lengthwise, seeded and sliced ¼ inch thick
Minced chives or parsley (garnish)

In large skillet bring broth, soy sauce and scallions to a boil. Stir in pork and simmer for 5 minutes. Stir in cucumbers and simmer for 3 minutes, or until cucumbers are crisp-tender. Garnish with chives or parsley.

FRIED RICE

(color plate 3)

3 tablespoons oil	5 cups cooked rice
4 eggs, slightly beaten	½ teaspoon salt
¾ cup chopped onion	¼ teaspoon garlic powder
1 cup frozen peas, thawed	Dash of pepper
1 cup chopped cooked ham	2 tablespoons soy sauce

In large skillet heat 2 tablespoons of the oil. Add eggs and cook and stir until set. Remove from skillet and set aside. Add remaining tablespoon of oil to skillet. Add onion, peas and ham. Stir-fry for 2 minutes. Stir in eggs and remaining ingredients. Heat through. Serve hot.

PORK CHOP SUEY

1½ pounds lean pork, shredded	2 tablespoons cornstarch
2 tablespoons peanut oil	3 tablespoons soy sauce
4 scallions, slivered	¼ teaspoon salt
3 stalks celery, sliced	¼ teaspoon pepper
1 1-pound can bean sprouts, drained	Rice
1 cup chicken broth	

Sauté the pork in the oil for 2 minutes while stirring. Add the scallions, celery and bean sprouts. Mix well. Add the broth and simmer, covered, for 5 minutes. Mix the cornstarch with a little water and stir in with the soy sauce, salt and pepper. Cook only until thickened, about 3 minutes. Serve with rice.

CRAB-PORK-PEPPER WEDGES

(color plate 3)

¾ pound ground lean pork (1½ cups)	2 tablespoons soy sauce
1 5½-ounce can crabmeat, drained and chopped	4 large green peppers, halved lengthwise, seeded, then cut crosswise into thirds
½ cup minced water chestnuts	
1 2-ounce can minced mushrooms	¼ cup peas for garnish (optional)
¼ cup minced scallions	

Mix well pork, crabmeat, water chestnuts, mushrooms, scallions and soy sauce. Fill each pepper piece with 1 tablespoon of the meat mixture. Garnish with peas. Place on large plate on top of 2 small heatproof bowls (glass custard cups work well) in large pot or steamer. Add water to within 2 inches of plate. Cover and bring to a boil. Place peppers on plate. Cover pot and steam for 40 minutes. Check water level occasionally, adding more if necessary. Serve hot with soy sauce on the side.

SWEET AND SOUR CHICKEN

(color plate 3)

2 tablespoons oil
1 3½-pound broiler-fryer cut up
1 large green pepper, seeded and cut in strips
1 onion, sliced
2 carrots, sliced diagonally (½ cup)
1 14-ounce bottle catsup
1 20-ounce can pineapple chunks in own juice, drained (reserve ½ cup juice)

⅓ cup cider vinegar
3 tablespoons sugar
1 teaspoon dry mustard
½ to 1 teaspoon chopped fresh ginger
1 medium-sized tomato, cut into chunks
2 tablespoons cornstarch blended with ¼ cup water
2 tablespoons soy sauce

In a large skillet heat the oil and brown the chicken on all sides. Remove with a slotted spoon and set aside. Add green pepper, onion and carrots to skillet and stir-fry for 2 minutes. Add catsup, pineapple juice, vinegar, sugar, mustard, ginger and chicken. Cover and simmer for 35 minutes, or until chicken is tender. Skim off fat. Add tomato, pineapple chunks and cornstarch-soy mixture. Stir until blended through and sauce has thickened.

HOT BUFFET
Vegetarian

Cheddar Cheese Soup
Tomato Aspic Ring with Egg Salad
Stuffed Cabbage
Vegetable Curry with Rice
Chutney (optional)
Mushroom Onion Pasta
Apple, Pear and Cheese Salad
Honey Pumpkin Pie

CHEDDAR CHEESE SOUP

2 medium-sized onions, sliced thin
3 tablespoons butter or margarine
4 tablespoons flour
1 teaspoon dry mustard
⅛ teaspoon hot pepper sauce
2 cups hot water
1 tablespoon Worcestershire sauce
2 large stalks celery, sliced thin

4 cups milk
8 ounces coarsely shredded sharp
    Cheddar cheese (1½ cups)
Salt
Sliced radishes, chopped green pepper,
    toasted slivered almonds or
    croutons (garnish)

In a 3-quart heavy saucepan sauté onion in butter or margarine until golden and tender. Blend in flour and mustard. Gradually stir in hot pepper sauce and water until thickened, then the Worcestershire sauce and celery. Cover and simmer for 15 minutes or until celery is tender. Add milk and heat almost to boiling. Stir in cheese until melted. Season to taste with salt. Serve topped with one or several of the garnishes.

TOMATO ASPIC RING WITH EGG SALAD

1 quart tomato or mixed vegetable
    juice, or a combination
1 tablespoon minced onion
2 tablespoons minced celery
½ teaspoon salt
¼ teaspoon pepper
1 teaspoon sugar
1 teaspoon dried basil or thyme or 1
    tablespoon fresh
2 envelopes gelatin
¼ cup water

4 hard-cooked eggs, chopped
2 scallions, chopped
1 green pepper, seeded and chopped
1 10-ounce package frozen artichoke
    hearts or 1 8-ounce can, cut in
    halves
½ cup Mayonnaise (see page 154 for
    recipe)
2 teaspoons lemon juice
Lemon wedges

Simmer the juice with onion, celery, salt, pepper, sugar and the herb. Soften the gelatin in the water and add the juice. Heat and stir until the gelatin is dissolved. Cool and pour into a 1½-quart ring mold. Cool until springy. Chill. Combine the eggs, scallions, green pepper and artichoke hearts with ⅓ cup of the mayonnaise and lemon juice. Chill. Turn out the mold and put the egg salad in the center. Garnish with the remaining mayonnaise and the lemon wedges.

STUFFED CABBAGE

2 medium-sized onions, chopped
1 cup hulled sunflower seeds
3 tablespoons oil
2 medium-sized apples, peeled, cored
    and coarsely chopped
3 cups cooked brown rice

1 cup raisins
½ teaspoon salt
½ teaspoon cinnamon
12 large cabbage leaves
1 15-ounce can tomato sauce
1 cup plain yogurt

In a large skillet sauté onion and sunflower seeds in oil until seeds are lightly browned and onion is tender. Add apples and sauté for 3 minutes. Remove from heat and stir in rice, raisins, salt and cinnamon. Turn into a bowl and set aside. Cook cabbage leaves in boiling water just until limp enough to handle, then drain. Cut out hard center rib in each leaf. Place ¼ cup filling at base of each leaf, fold in sides and roll up. In same skillet pour tomato sauce. Place filled rolls, seam side down, in skillet. Simmer, covered, for 30 minutes, or until cabbage is tender. Serve warm, topped with yogurt.

VEGETABLE CURRY

1 large onion, sliced thin	1 pound green beans, cut up
2 tablespoons butter	3 green peppers, seeded and cut up
2 teaspoons grated fresh ginger or	1 large eggplant, cubed
1 teaspoon ground	2 cups milk
1 tablespoon curry powder	¼ cup chopped parsley
1 tablespoon salt	2 tablespoons flour
½ teaspoon sugar	2 tablespoons toasted shredded
¼ teaspoon paprika	coconut
4 large potatoes, peeled and cubed	Rice
6 carrots, scraped and cut up	

Sauté the onion in butter for 2 minutes. Add the seasonings and stir well. Add the vegetables and milk. Simmer, covered, for about 15 minutes, or until the vegetables are tender. Add the parsley. Make a thin paste of the flour and a little milk. Stir into the curry and simmer for 5 minutes, stirring occasionally. Sprinkle the top with coconut. Serve with rice. Serves 10 to 12.

MUSHROOM ONION PASTA

2 large Bermuda or Spanish onions	1½ pounds thin Italian spaghetti or
2 tablespoons butter	small shells
2 tablespoons oil	½ cup cream
¾ pound mushrooms	¼ cup grated Parmesan cheese

Slice the onion and sauté in 1 tablespoon of the butter and 1 tablespoon of the oil until tender. Stir and do not let brown. Slice the mushrooms thin; a processor slicing blade is fine for this. Sauté the mushrooms in the remaining butter and oil in a separate pan, stirring. Do not brown. Add the mushrooms to the onion. Meanwhile, cook the pasta in a large amount of boiling salted water for about 5 minutes. Drain. Add the cream and cheese to the onion-mushroom mixture and toss with the pasta. Serve hot or at room temperature. Serves 10 as an appetizer.

APPLE, PEAR AND CHEESE SALAD

3 apples, cored and peeled
3 pears, cored and peeled
½ pound Swiss cheese

1 tablespoon lemon juice
⅓ cup Mayonnaise (see page 154 for recipe)

Cut the apples and pears in cubes. Cut the cheese in cubes about the same size as the fruit. Combine the lemon juice with the mayonnaise and pour over the salad at once. The fruit will darken if you let it stand undressed.

HONEY PUMPKIN PIE

1½ cups canned pumpkin
½ cup honey
2 teaspoons grated orange peel
½ teaspoon cinnamon
½ teaspoon salt
¼ teaspoon nutmeg

¼ teaspoon ginger
½ teaspoon vanilla
2 eggs, beaten
1 cup evaporated milk
1 9-inch frozen pie shell
1 egg white, slightly beaten

In large bowl, combine all ingredients, except last two. Beat until well blended. Brush pie shell with egg white and bake at 425°F. for 5 minutes. Remove from oven, pour in filling and bake for 45 minutes, or until firm. Serve warm or cool.

HOT BUFFET

Steamed Brook Trout or Smelts

Boeuf Bourguignon

French Bread or Hard Rolls

Puree of Green Peas

Wax Beans, Italian Style

Endive and Lettuce Salad with Pimento

Pears Hélène with Ice Cream

STEAMED BROOK TROUT OR SMELTS

8 (about ½ pound) trout or smelts
¼ cup melted butter
1 teaspoon lemon juice

1 tablespoon minced dill or parsley
1 teaspoon salt
Lemon wedges

Leave the heads and tails on the fish. Place each on a square of foil large enough to enclose the fish. Brush with butter mixed with lemon juice. Sprinkle with dill or parsley and salt. Fold the foil over envelope fashion so no juice can escape. Steam in a 400°F. oven for 25 minutes. Serve in the foil. Let each help himself to a fish and roll it out on his plate when seated. If you can't get large smelts, put 2 in each package.

BOEUF BOURGUIGNON

4 pounds top round, cut into ¾- to
   1-inch cubes
Flour
3 tablespoons butter (or part oil)
3 tablespoons brandy, warmed
6 slices bacon, cut up
2 medium-sized onions, chopped
2 large carrots, scraped and chopped
1 teaspoon salt
½ teaspoon pepper

⅛ teaspoon sugar
1 tablespoon chopped parsley
1 cup water
2 cups dry red wine
Bouquet garni (3 sprigs parsley, 1 bay
   leaf and 1 sprig thyme)
1 tablespoon tomato puree
1 pound mushrooms (optional)
1½ pounds small white onions,
   parboiled (optional)

Sprinkle the meat with a very little flour and brown on all sides in butter or oil. Add the brandy and ignite. After the flames die out, transfer the meat to a casserole. Sauté the bacon in the same skillet, but do not brown. Remove the bacon and add to the meat. Brown the onion and carrots in the drippings. Stir in 2 tablespoons flour. Add the salt, pepper, sugar and parsley. When the flour is tan, stir in the water and pour it over the meat. Add the wine and bouquet garni. Add a little water, wine or broth if the liquid does not cover the meat and vegetables. Simmer, covered, for about 2 hours. Remove the bouquet garni and stir in the tomato puree. If you want mushrooms and/or onions, sauté in a little butter, add to the casserole and simmer for 10 minutes. Serves 10 to 12.

PUREE OF GREEN PEAS

4 pounds fresh peas, or 3 10-ounce
   packages frozen
¼ cup water
½ cup butter, melted

1 teaspoon salt
¼ teaspoon pepper
⅓ cup cream

Cook the peas in water until tender; if using frozen peas, follow package instructions. Put into a processor or blender with the butter, salt and pepper. Puree. Reheat, stirring in the cream and beat until light and fluffy. If using a blender, you may have to add the cream while blending in order to make a smooth puree.

WAX BEANS, ITALIAN STYLE

3 pounds fresh wax beans, or 3 10-ounce packages frozen cut	½ teaspoon sugar
3 tablespoons olive oil	1 teaspoon salt
1 clove garlic, crushed	¼ teaspoon pepper
1 cup beef broth or consommé	1 large or 2 medium tomatoes, peeled and chopped
1 tablespoon minced parsley	

Trim the ends and cut the fresh beans into 1-inch pieces or French cut them. If using frozen beans, thaw. Toss in hot oil with the garlic. Add the remaining ingredients except the tomatoes. Cover tightly and steam for 15 minutes. Add the tomatoes and cook about 5 or 6 minutes, stirring several times. Do not overcook. Taste for seasoning. The amount of salt depends upon the seasoning in the broth.

ENDIVE AND LETTUCE SALAD WITH PIMENTO

2 pounds Belgian endive	½ cup pimentos, cut into strips
1 large head Boston lettuce or 2 heads Bibb	⅓ cup French Dressing (see page 155 for recipe)

Wash and dry the endive and lettuce. Cut the endive across the heads in slices about ¾ inch thick. Break the lettuce into bite-sized pieces. Place in a bowl with pimentos and mix gently so the endive will not fall completely apart. Pour the French dressing over just before serving.

PEARS HÉLÈNE WITH ICE CREAM

6 large pears	2 teaspoons vanilla
2 cups sugar	1 to 2 quarts vanilla ice cream
3 cups water	Chocolate Sauce

Peel, halve and core the pears. Meanwhile, boil the sugar and water for about 5 minutes. Add pears and simmer about 10 to 15 minutes or until tender. The time depends upon the size of the pears and their ripeness. Add vanilla and chill. Place the pears, cut-side down, on top of ice cream and pour the chocolate sauce over. (For recipes for chocolate sauces, see pages 77 and 156.) Serves 6 to 12. Use 1 quart ice cream for 6, 2 for 12.

HOT BUFFET

Artichokes Vinaigrette
Chicken Kabobs
Lamb Curry
Rice Pilaf
Summer Squash
Herbed Scalloped Tomatoes
Coleslaw with Grapes
Frozen Maple Mousse
Sour Cream Drop Cookies

ARTICHOKES VINAIGRETTE

8 artichokes

½ to 1 cup Vinaigrette Dressing (see page 155 for recipe)

Trim the stems so that artichokes will stand upright on a plate. Pull off any small discolored outside leaves. You may trim off the tops with scissors, if you wish. It makes them look nice and easier to hold the leaves when eating. Boil in a pot of water almost to cover. Add 1 tablespoon of salt and 1 tablespoon of vinegar per quart; or you may steam them on the rack of a steamer. Test for doneness by pulling out a leaf; if it pulls out easily, the artichoke is done. They take about 30 minutes to cook, boiled or steamed. Drain upside-down. Chill. Serve the dressing in small side dishes.

CHICKEN KABOBS

(Yakitori)

3½ to 4 pounds chicken breasts or thighs
½ cup sake or sweet sherry

¼ cup soy sauce
1 tablespoon sugar
1 tablespoon peanut or vegetable oil

Cut the chicken into about 1-inch cubes and thread onto 8 skewers. Mix the remaining ingredients and dip the skewered chicken into the sauce. Broil for 10 minutes. Dip in the sauce again and broil for 10 minutes on the other side.

LAMB CURRY

4 pounds lean lamb, cut into 1-inch cubes	1 tablespoon salt
Flour	1 bay leaf, crumbled
½ cup butter	1 clove garlic, crushed
1½ cups finely chopped onion	¼ teaspoon thyme
½ cup chopped celery	Dash of pepper
3 cups chicken broth	1 cup peeled, cored and diced apple
1 cup consommé	1 cup seedless raisins
2 tablespoons curry powder	1 ripe banana, mashed
	3 tablespoons chutney

Dredge the lamb in flour and brown well in the butter in a heavy pot. Add the onion and celery. Stir in the chicken broth and consommé. Add the curry powder, salt, bay leaf, garlic, thyme and pepper. Cover and simmer for about 1 hour or until the meat is almost tender. Remove the meat and set aside. Add the apple, raisins, banana and chutney to the broth. Adjust the seasonings; you may want more curry. Mix 3 to 4 tablespoons flour into a smooth paste with water. Stir into the sauce and cook gently until thickened. Add the lamb and continue cooking until very tender, about 20 minutes. Serve with condiments. See page 154 for a list of suggested condiments. Serves 12.

RICE PILAF

2 cups rice	1 teaspoon salt
2 tablespoons minced onion	3½ cups chicken broth
⅓ cup butter	

Sauté the rice and onion in butter in a heavy saucepan, stirring. Cook until straw color. Add the salt and broth. Cover and simmer for 15 minutes without stirring. The rice should be tender and the liquid absorbed.

SUMMER SQUASH

6 to 8 young summer squash, sliced	1 tablespoon minced onion
3 tablespoons butter	¼ teaspoon oregano or basil
1 teaspoon salt	

Sauté the squash in butter with the salt, onion and oregano for 3 to 4 minutes, or until tender. Shake the pan occasionally to keep it from sticking.

Variation: Add 1½ cups diced or canned tomatoes and ¼ teaspoon sugar. Reheat.

HERBED SCALLOPED TOMATOES

6 cups canned tomatoes
3 cups packaged stuffing mix
2 small onions, chopped fine
2 tablespoons sugar
½ teaspoon salt

½ teaspoon nutmeg
½ teaspoon oregano
¼ teaspoon pepper
¼ teaspoon ground rosemary
¼ cup butter

Mix together all ingredients, except ⅓ cup of the stuffing mix and the butter, in a buttered 2-quart casserole. Top the casserole with the remaining stuffing mix and dot well with the butter. Bake at 375°F. for 45 minutes. Serves 8 to 10.

COLESLAW WITH GRAPES

1 large head cabbage, shredded
¾ cup Mayonnaise (see page 154 for recipe)

1 teaspoon sugar
3 cups seedless white grapes

Mix the cabbage with ½ cup of the dressing and sugar. Add more dressing, if the coleslaw is not moist enough. Stir in the grapes gently as they crush easily. Chill.

FROZEN MAPLE MOUSSE

1½ cups maple syrup

3 cups heavy cream

Heat the syrup and remove any scum from the top. Chill. Whip the cream and combine with the syrup. Spoon into a serving dish and freeze at once until firm. Serves 10 to 12.

SOUR CREAM DROP COOKIES

¼ cup butter
1½ cups sugar
2 eggs, well beaten
2½ cups flour
¼ teaspoon salt

1 teaspoon baking soda
1 cup sour cream
1 teaspoon nutmeg
Raisins (optional)

Cream the butter with the sugar. Add the eggs and beat until light. Sift the flour, salt and baking soda together. Add to the creamed mixture alternately with the sour cream. Mix well. Flavor with nutmeg. Drop by tablespoonfuls several inches apart onto a greased baking sheet. Put a large seeded raisin in the center of each, if you wish. Bake at 375°F. for 12 to 15 minutes. Yield: 2 dozen.

HOT BUFFET

Cup of Jellied Consommé
Pot Roast (Sauerbraten)
Chicken Breasts in Foil
Mashed Potatoes
Green Bean Casserole
Tomato Aspic with Blue Cheese Dressing
Baked Spiced Peaches
Brownies

POT ROAST

(Sauerbraten)

1 4-pound piece top sirloin of beef,
   boned and rolled
2 teaspoons salt
¼ teaspoon pepper
2 cups water
2 cups vinegar
2 large onions, sliced
3 bay leaves
6 celery tops
12 peppercorns
1 large carrot, sliced
¼ teaspoon thyme
4 cloves
Flour
2 tablespoons oil
⅓ cup seedless raisins, plumped in
   boiling water
5 gingersnaps, crushed

Rub the beef with the salt and pepper. Place in a large bowl with the water, vinegar, onion, bay leaves, celery, peppercorns, carrot, thyme and cloves. Cover with plastic wrap and marinate in the refrigerator for 2 or 3 days, turning about twice a day. When ready to cook, dust the meat with seasoned flour. Sear quickly on all sides in the oil. Add the marinade, vegetables and all, cover and simmer slowly for about 3 hours, or until tender. Add more water, if necessary. When the meat is tender, lift out onto a hot platter and keep it warm. Strain the juices. Add the raisins and the gingersnaps. Cook, stirring constantly, until smooth and thickened. Add more seasoning, if necessary. Pour part of the gravy over the meat and serve the rest on the side. Serves 8 to 12.

CHICKEN BREASTS IN FOIL

4 chicken breasts, halved
2 bay leaves, crumbled
1 cup chicken broth
1 tablespoon minced parsley

¼ teaspoon tarragon
1 teaspoon salt
¼ teaspoon pepper

Place each breast on a piece of foil. Combine all the remaining ingredients and divide among the chicken breasts. Fold the foil over each, envelope fashion. Make sure no liquid can escape. Bake at 375°F. for 40 minutes, or cook on the rack of a steamer. Serve in the foil so each may open his own package, enjoy the aroma and get all the juices.

CHICKEN BREASTS WITH MUSHROOMS

Add ½ pound sliced mushrooms to the breasts and proceed as for Chicken Breasts in Foil.

MASHED POTATOES

8 potatoes
1 teaspoon salt
¼ teaspoon pepper

⅓ cup butter
½ cup half-and-half, heated

Boil the potatoes in their jackets in salted water until quite tender, about 30 minutes. Peel while still hot and put through a ricer or processor. Add salt, pepper, butter and ⅓ cup of the half-and-half. Beat or process until fluffy, adding more half-and-half and salt to taste. If you cannot serve them at once, pile into a buttered casserole and keep warm in a low oven.

GREEN BEAN CASSEROLE

2½ to 3 pounds young green beans
3 tablespoons chopped shallots or
   scallions
2 tablespoons melted butter

1 teaspoon lemon juice
1 teaspoon salt
½ teaspoon pepper
¼ teaspoon oregano

Snip the ends off the beans and place them, all lying in one direction, in a shallow ovenproof dish. Sprinkle with the remaining ingredients. Place on the rack of a steamer and steam for 20 minutes. Serve in the casserole.

TOMATO ASPIC

1 quart mixed vegetable or tomato
   juice
1 tablespoon minced celery
2 tablespoons minced scallions or
   onion
1 teaspoon sugar

½ teaspoon salt
¼ teaspoon pepper
½ teaspoon oregano
2 teaspoons lemon juice
2 envelopes gelatin
¼ cup cold water

Heat the juice with all the ingredients except the gelatin and water. Soften the gelatin in cold water and stir into the hot tomato mixture until the gelatin is dissolved. Cool. Pour into a 1½-quart ring mold or other mold. Chill until firm. Turn out on a cold platter. Have dressing available on the buffet: Blue Cheese Dressing (recipe follows). You may fill the center with any cooked vegetable or watercress.

BLUE CHEESE DRESSING

Soften 4 ounces blue, Roquefort or Gorgonzola cheese at room temperature and mash it before stirring into French Dressing. (See page 155 for recipe.)

BAKED SPICED PEACHES

8 peaches, halved and pits removed
⅓ cup maple syrup
¼ cup light brown sugar, packed
½ teaspoon cinnamon

2 tablespoons butter or margarine,
   melted
Frozen whipped topping, partially
   thawed, or whipped cream (garnish)

Place peach halves, hollow side up, in a shallow baking dish or 9-inch pie pan. Drizzle with maple syrup and sprinkle with mixture of sugar and cinnamon. Add the butter or margarine and bake at 325°F. for 30 minutes. Cool and top each peach half with a dab of whipped topping or cream.

BROWNIES

1 cup flour
¾ teaspoon baking powder
¼ teaspoon salt
3 ounces unsweetened chocolate
½ cup butter

1½ cups sugar
3 eggs, beaten
¾ cup coarsely chopped pecans
1 teaspoon vanilla

Sift the flour, baking powder and salt together. Melt the chocolate and butter in a double boiler. Gradually stir the sugar into the eggs and add to the melted chocolate mixture. Blend in the flour and then the pecans and vanilla. Bake in a greased 9 x 9 x 2-inch pan at 350°F. for 30 to 40 minutes. Cut into rectangular pieces and cool on a rack. Yield: about 3 dozen brownies.

HOT BUFFET

Vegetarian

Vegetable Tamale Pie
Tofu (bean curd)-Watercress Salad
Squash Ring
Three-Bean Salad
Tomatoes Stuffed with Curried Rice
Baked Alaska with Chocolate Rum Sauce

VEGETABLE TAMALE PIE

2 medium-sized onions, chopped
1 medium-sized green pepper, seeded
  and chopped
2 cloves garlic, minced
3 tablespoons oil
1 (1 pound) can tomatoes, cut up
1 tablespoon chili powder
½ cup chopped stuffed green olives
  (24 small)

2 1-pound cans red kidney beans,
  drained
2 17-ounce cans whole-kernel corn,
  drained
1 12-ounce package corn muffin mix
⅔ cup milk
1 egg, slightly beaten
¾ cup shredded Cheddar cheese

In a large, deep ovenproof skillet sauté onion, green pepper and garlic in oil until onion is tender. Add tomatoes, chili powder and olives. Simmer, stirring occasionally, for 10 minutes. Remove from heat and stir in beans and corn. Prepare muffin mix according to package instructions, using milk and egg. Spoon over bean mixture and sprinkle with cheese. Bake at 400°F. for 20 minutes, or until lightly browned and pick inserted in center comes out clean. Let stand for 10 minutes before serving.

TOFU (BEAN CURD)-WATERCRESS SALAD

2 cakes (3 x 3 x 1½ inch) tofu
  (bean curd)
2 bunches watercress
½ to 1 teaspoon soy sauce

⅓ cup French Dressing (see page 155
  for recipe)
Pieces of pimento for garnish
  (optional)

Cut the tofu into ½-inch pieces. Remove the heavy stems from the watercress and chop coarsely, reserving 6 or 8 sprigs for garnish. Add soy sauce to the French Dressing and toss thoroughly with the cress. Put the cress in a serving bowl and fold in the tofu. Toss gently so you won't mash the tofu. Arrange the reserved watercress sprigs around the edge. Sprinkle top of the salad with pimentos, if you wish.

SQUASH RING

2 10-ounce packages frozen squash
2 tablespoons minced onion
2 tablespoons butter
1 teaspoon salt

¼ teaspoon pepper
Dash of hot pepper sauce
4 eggs, well beaten

Cook the squash according to package instructions. Season with the onion, butter, salt, pepper and hot pepper sauce. Fold in the eggs and pour into a well-greased 6-cup ring mold. Bake in a pan of hot water in a 350°F. oven for 1 hour. Unmold onto a hot plate and serve with a green vegetable such as peas or green beans in the center. You may make this in a regular mold and serve it plain.

THREE-BEAN SALAD

1 pound fresh green beans, or 1
  10-ounce package frozen
1 pound fresh wax beans or 1
  10-ounce package frozen
1 10-ounce package frozen small
  limas

4 scallions, chopped
½ cup French Dressing (see page 155
  for recipe)
1 tablespoon chopped fresh basil, or
  1 teaspoon dry
Salad greens (optional)

Cut the green and wax beans, unless they are very young. Cook in salted water until crisp-tender. If using frozen, cook according to package instructions. Drain. Combine all the beans with the scallions. Stir in the French Dressing and the basil. Chill. Serve with greens, if you wish.

TOMATOES STUFFED WITH CURRIED RICE

4 large tomatoes
1 teaspoon salt
⅛ teaspoon pepper
¼ teaspoon sugar
¾ cup finely chopped green pepper

2 teaspoons curry powder
1⅓ cups soft bread crumbs
4 cups cooked rice
Buttered crumbs for topping

Slice the tops off the tomatoes, scoop out the insides and mash with a fork. Season with the salt, pepper and sugar. Add the green pepper and curry. Heat together and blend in the soft crumbs and rice. Stuff the tomatoes with this mixture. Sprinkle with the buttered crumbs. Broil under low heat for 10 minutes, or until the tomatoes are just tender.

BAKED ALASKA WITH CHOCOLATE RUM SAUCE

(color plate 8)

½ cup butter or margarine
3 ounces unsweetened chocolate
2 eggs, slightly beaten
1 cup sugar
½ teaspoon salt

1 teaspoon vanilla
⅔ cup flour
½ gallon coffee or other ice cream
Meringue (see page 12 for recipe)
Chocolate Rum Sauce (recipe follows)

In small saucepan over low heat stir butter or margarine and chocolate until melted and smooth. Transfer to a large bowl and cool slightly. Add eggs, sugar and salt. Beat about 3 minutes, or until thickened. Beat in vanilla. Stir in flour just until blended. Spread evenly in a well-greased 8- or 9-inch square pan. Bake at 350°F. for 30 minutes or until pick inserted in center comes out clean. Cool in pan on rack for 5 minutes, then invert onto rack. Cool thoroughly and cut in half. Halve ice cream lengthwise. Put a half on each cake. Place in freezer while making meringue. Place Alaska on foil-lined cutting board. Spread meringue to cover Alaskas completely and seal in ice cream. Bake at 425°F. for 5 minutes, or until lightly browned. Serve immediately from board or serving dish with Chocolate Rum Sauce.

CHOCOLATE RUM SAUCE

2 ounces unsweetened chocolate
½ cup water
½ cup sugar

2 tablespoons butter or margarine
3 tablespoons dark rum

In small saucepan over low heat stir chocolate and water until chocolate melts and mixture is smooth. Add sugar and stir in butter or margarine until melted. Stir in rum. Serve at room temperature. Yield: 1 cup.

III

COLD BUFFETS

Cold food is a pleasure in any kind of weather. It is ideal on a buffet when cooking ahead is an important consideration, as it often is these days. The food is not only cooked ahead, but presented ahead—far enough so that the hostess is free to join her guests at bridge or a movie. If the buffet has to wait for several hours, it should be protected by a cover, which is whisked off by the magician-hostess.

The cold spread means that everyone does not need to rush to the buffet at the same time, that latecomers are not a major problem. Soups are often better cold than hot and most important, there is a surprisingly large number of excellent *cold* main dishes.

This chapter has everything from a spectacular *smörgåsbord* or a dramatic whole salmon in aspic to a simple but delicious chicken, meat or fish meal salad.

COLD BUFFET

Smörgäsbord

The Scandinavian word means "spread bread on a table." Actually it is a festive buffet for a large honored group. Traditionally, there are a number of open-face sandwiches, many fishes, some meats, vegetables, pâtés, salads, cheeses and often hot Swedish meat balls.

Make the dishes as attractive as you can, garnishing them with fresh dill, when available, parsley, chives, red or green peppers and pimento.

For your *smörgäsbord*, choose as many dishes as you like from the following menu list (some, such as sardines and herring in sauce can be purchased), keeping a balance and variety in mind.

MENU LIST

Herring Salad with Beets and Potatoes
Herring in Sour Cream or Wine Sauce
Herring and Beet Salad
Pickled Herring
Pickled Beets
Marinated Mussels
Large or Medium Shrimp
Shrimp with Apple
Baby Shrimp with Dill on Shredded Lettuce
Smoked Salmon on Cream Cheese on Bread Rounds
Sardines in their can or on Toast Strips
Sardines on Dark Bread Fingers
Anchovy Fillets on Toast Pieces
Salmon in Foil
Smoked Eels
Ham Mousse Mold
Sliced Sausages
Cold-Cut Cornucopias
Fresh Tongue in Aspic
Liver Loaf

Hard-Cooked Egg Slices Topped with Rolled Anchovies
Hard-Cooked Egg Slices on Sliced Tomatoes
Radishes
Celery
Potato and Green Bean Salad
Chicken Cucumber Salad
Pâté
Deviled Eggs with Ham
Deviled Eggs with Cucumbers
Scandinavian Cucumbers
Swedish Meat Balls (not on a cold table but can be on a chafing dish on the side)

ALWAYS

Breads: Thick Dry Toast, Swedish Rye, Pumpernickel, Finn Crisp or other Rye Crisps and butter
Sauces: Mayonnaise, Mustard, Dill Mayonnaise
Cookies, if you wish: Almond, Ginger, Sugar Cookies and Sand Tarts (see page 135 for recipe)
Assorted Cheeses

HERRING SALAD WITH BEETS AND POTATOES

1 1-pound can diced beets
3 cups diced cooked potatoes
⅓ cup chopped onion
3 hard-cooked eggs, chopped
2½ cups (2 8-ounce jars) chopped
  marinated herring

1 cup Mayonnaise (see page 154 for
  recipe)
2 tablespoons sour cream
1 apple, peeled and grated

Drain the beets and reserve the juice. Combine the beets, potatoes, onion and eggs with the herring. Combine the mayonnaise, sour cream, ½ cup juice from the beets and the apple. Pour over the salad and chill for several hours.

PICKLED BEETS

2 bunches beets, very small, if
  available, or about 10–12 medium
  to large
1 large sweet onion, sliced very thin
¾ cup vinegar

½ cup water
½ cup sugar
1 teaspoon salt
4 cloves

Cut the leaves from the beets leaving 1 inch of stem. Boil until tender, about 40 minutes. Cool, cut off stems and slice thin. If using tiny beets, leave them whole. Place in a bowl or jar with the onion. Mix the remaining ingredients and pour over, stirring to ensure all beets being covered. Let stand for 6 hours or overnight. You may let stand several days, if you wish. Drain. Serves 10 to 12.

HERRING AND BEET SALAD

2 8-ounce jars herring
Canned beets (1 small-sized can)
3 dill pickles, diced
½ cup sour cream

⅓ cup Mayonnaise (see page 154 for
  recipe)
Salad greens (optional)

Drain and dice the herring, reserving the juice. Drain the beets, reserving the juice. Mix the herring and beets with the pickles. Combine 2 tablespoons herring juice, 2 tablespoons beet juice, sour cream and mayonnaise. Pour over the salad and mix thoroughly. Refrigerate for 3 or more hours. Serve with greens, if you wish.

HERRING SALAD

2 or 3 medium-sized salt herring
3 cups diced beets
1½ cups diced cooked potatoes
3 hard-cooked eggs, chopped, or 3
  apples, peeled and chopped

3 tablespoons Mayonnaise (see page
  154 for recipe)
¼ cup cream

Soak the herring overnight in cold water to cover. Drain, remove skin and bones and cut into small pieces. Mix with the beets and potatoes and eggs or apples. Combine the mayonnaise and cream and pour over. Toss gently. Serves 12.

MARINATED MUSSELS

8 dozen large mussels	¼ cup olive oil
1 cup white wine	2 teaspoons lemon juice
1 slice white bread	½ teaspoon salt
2 cloves garlic, crushed or minced fine	½ teaspoon pepper

Steam the mussels in white wine until they open. When cool, remove them from their shells, put into a bowl and chill. Remove the crust from the bread, pull apart and mix with the garlic. Work in the oil, lemon juice, salt and pepper and ½ cup of the liquid the mussels were steamed in. Pour over the mussels and marinate for several hours or overnight in the refrigerator. Pour off part of the marinade before serving. The mussels should be wet but not covered with marinade. Serves 8 to 10.

SHRIMP WITH APPLE

3 pounds shrimp	¾ cup sour cream
4 large apples, peeled and cored	Juice of 1 lemon
Shredded iceberg lettuce, about 1 small head	1 to 2 tablespoons catsup (optional)
¾ cup Mayonnaise (see page 154 for recipe)	

Simmer the shrimp until they turn pink, about 3 minutes after the water boils. Peel and slice lengthwise, unless the shrimp are very small. Cut the apples about the size of the shrimp. Combine the shrimp, apples and lettuce. Mix the mayonnaise, sour cream and lemon juice and add enough catsup to make the dressing a pale pink if you wish. Pour over the salad, toss and chill.

SALMON IN FOIL

1 3½-pound piece of salmon	Few sprigs parsley
1 teaspoon lemon juice	½ cup white wine or dry vermouth
Few celery leaves	Lemon wedges

Place the salmon on a piece of foil and sprinkle with the lemon juice. Add the celery and parsley and pour the wine over. Fold up the foil and seal securely. Bake at 375°F. for 45 minutes. To serve the salmon cold, cool slightly in the foil before removing any skin and bones. Chill before serving. Serve with lemon wedges.

HAM MOUSSE MOLD

1½ envelopes gelatin
¼ cup cold water
½ cup pineapple juice

4 cups ground ham
1 teaspoon prepared mustard
1 cup cream, whipped

Soften the gelatin in water and heat with the pineapple juice to dissolve the gelatin. Add to the ham and mustard and cool. Fold in the whipped cream and spoon into a 1½-quart mold. Chill until firm, about 3 to 4 hours. Turn out on a cold platter.

COLD-CUT CORNUCOPIAS

2½ pounds sliced cold cooked beef, ham and/or bologna
2½ cups egg salad with 1 tablespoon prepared mustard

or
2½ cups Cooked Vegetable Salad (see pages 60 and 12 for recipes)

Roll the meat into cornucopias, fastening with a toothpick after filling. Beef is good filled with vegetable salad. Ham goes particularly well with egg salad to which you have added the mustard. Any filling can be put into bologna.

FRESH TONGUE IN ASPIC

1 4- to 5-pound fresh beef tongue
2 teaspoons salt
2 tablespoons butter
1 cup water
½ cup white wine

Bouquet garni (parsley sprigs, a celery stalk with leaves and 2 scallions)
1 envelope gelatin
¼ cup cold water
Greens (garnish)

Boil the tongue in water to cover, adding the salt, for about 2 hours or until the skin is loose enough to pull off. Place the peeled tongue in a pot with the remaining ingredients except the gelatin and water. If the liquid does not cover the tongue, add a little of the water the tongue was cooked in. Cover and simmer until the tongue is very tender, about 1 hour. Remove the tongue and cool. Reduce the broth to about half. Soften the gelatin in the cold water and pour into the broth. Heat and stir until the gelatin is dissolved. Cool until springy. Trim and slice the tongue onto a deep cold platter in slightly overlapping slices, or you may trim the tongue and leave it whole. Pour the syrupy broth over and chill. If you leave the tongue whole, pour only half the broth over, chill and then pour the remaining thickened broth over to coat thoroughly. Garnish the platter with parsley or other greens.

LIVER LOAF

1 pound liver, preferably beef or calf
2 large onions, cut up
5 anchovy fillets
½ pound salt pork
1 egg, beaten

½ cup milk
½ cup flour
½ teaspoon salt
¼ teaspoon pepper
6 slices bacon

Chop the liver, onion and anchovies in a processor. After a few seconds, scrape down the sides and add the salt pork and blend in for a few seconds. You may also do this in a food grinder. Add the egg to the milk and pour into the liver mixture. Blend in flour, salt and pepper, mixing thoroughly. Line a loaf pan with bacon, spoon in the liver and press down hard. Bake at 350°F. for 1 hour. Chill.

POTATO AND GREEN BEAN SALAD

(color plate 6, bottom)

2 pounds cooked cut green beans
5 warm cooked large potatoes, peeled
   and cubed (about 4 cups)
2 scallions, chopped
¼ cup oil
3 tablespoons white-wine vinegar
1 clove garlic, crushed (optional)

1 small red onion, sliced thin and
   broken into rings
½ teaspoon oregano
1 teaspoon salt
⅛ teaspoon pepper
Lettuce

Place beans, potatoes and scallions in a bowl. In jar mix well oil, vinegar, garlic, red onion, oregano, salt and pepper. Pour over vegetables. Toss gently to blend. Cover and chill for several hours or overnight. Serve in lettuce-lined bowl, if desired.

CHICKEN CUCUMBER SALAD

4 cups shredded cooked chicken
3 large cucumbers, peeled and
   shredded
3 scallions, minced

1 teaspoon Worcestershire sauce
1 teaspoon prepared mustard
¼ cup Lemon French Dressing (see
   page 155 for recipe)

Combine the chicken, cucumbers and scallions in a bowl. Add the Worcestershire sauce and mustard to the dressing and mix well. Pour over the salad, toss and chill.

DEVILED EGGS WITH HAM

Add ¾ cup minced ham to Deviled Eggs (see page 92 for recipe) and omit the curry. For a change, add 1 cup minced cucumbers instead of ham.

SCANDINAVIAN CUCUMBERS

4 to 5 cucumbers
¾ cup vinegar
¼ cup water
¼ cup sugar
½ teaspoon salt

2 tablespoons minced parsley or fresh
   dill
2 tablespoons minced chives or
   scallions (optional)

Slice the unpeeled cucumbers thinly. Combine the vinegar, water, sugar and salt. Blend thoroughly and pour over the cucumbers. Let stand for several hours. Drain and garnish with parsley or dill and chives, if you wish. Serves 10 to 12.

SWEDISH MEAT BALLS

3 large slices white bread
¾ cup milk
2 pounds lean ground beef (or try
   1⅓ pounds ground beef,
   ⅔ pound ground pork)
1 large onion, chopped fine

¼ cup butter
2 teaspoons salt
½ teaspoon pepper
½ teaspoon nutmeg (optional)
2 eggs, beaten

Soak the bread in the milk (if all the milk is absorbed, add a little more). Combine with the beef and/or pork. Sauté the onion in 2 tablespoons of the butter for 2 minutes and add to the meat, together with salt, pepper and the nutmeg, if you wish. Stir in the eggs. Blend thoroughly and form into small balls, about ½ inch in diameter. This is easier to do if you wet your hands. Sauté the balls in the remaining butter until brown, about 5 to 6 minutes. Shake the pan and do not cook too many at a time; add butter as needed. For a smörgåsbord you do not need a sauce, but you can make it by adding 2 tablespoons flour and ½ cup water. When it boils, stir in 1 cup sour cream to the juices in the pan. Reheat the balls gently in the sauce. Yield: about 80 meat balls.

COLD BUFFET

Mexican Escabeche
Platter of Assorted Cold Cuts
Chicken Breasts in Sauce
Macaroni Salad with Tomatoes
Asparagus Salad
Parfaits

MEXICAN ESCABECHE

4 pounds fish fillets (mackerel,
  snapper, flounder or pompano)
2 tablespoons lemon juice
⅔ cup olive oil
½ cup white wine vinegar
2 cloves garlic, minced
4 scallions, chopped

1 teaspoon salt
½ teaspoon pepper
½ teaspoon oregano
1 whole hot green or red pepper,
  seeded and cut in half
2 tablespoons capers
Shredded lettuce (optional)

Cut the fish into bite-sized pieces and sprinkle with the lemon juice. Heat 3 tablespoons oil and sauté the fish gently until lightly browned on both sides, about 1 minute. Transfer to a flat serving dish. Add the vinegar, garlic, salt, pepper, oregano and the hot pepper to the pan. Heat for a few minutes, add the remaining oil and capers and pour over the fish. Remove the pepper. Refrigerate overnight or longer. Serve on shredded lettuce. Serves 12.

CHICKEN BREASTS IN SAUCE

8 small boned half chicken breasts
3 tablespoons butter
3 tablespoons flour
1 cup chicken broth
1 cup cream

1 teaspoon salt
2 egg yolks, slightly beaten
2 tablespoons dark orange marmalade
  or chutney

The chicken breasts may be steamed or poached. When cool, put them on a platter. Melt the butter, blend in the flour and stir in the broth. Stir steadily while adding the cream.

Combine the eggs with a few tablespoons of cold liquid (broth, cream or milk) and stir into the sauce. Heat and stir until thickened, but do not boil. Chop any large pieces in the marmalade or chutney and stir in. Cool. Spoon over the chicken and chill for several hours or overnight.

MACARONI SALAD WITH TOMATOES

1 pound shell macaroni
1 bouillon cube or 1 teaspoon instant
  beef bouillon
¼ cup milk or water, hot
¾ cup Mayonnaise (see page 154 for
  recipe)
1 teaspoon lemon juice
½ teaspoon salt

¼ teaspoon pepper
1 teaspoon sugar
1 teaspoon dried basil or dill, or
  1 tablespoon chopped fresh
2 large or 3 medium-sized tomatoes,
  peeled and chopped
½ cup chopped raw or Bermuda onion
Minced parsley

Cook the macaroni according to package instructions. Drain and cool. Dissolve the bouillon in the hot liquid. Cool. Mix the mayonnaise with the lemon juice, salt, pepper, sugar and the herb. Stir in the bouillon. Pour over the macaroni and toss. Add the tomatoes and onion and toss again thoroughly but gently. Chill. Sprinkle with parsley.

ASPARAGUS SALAD

3 pounds fresh asparagus or 3
  (10-ounce) packages frozen
Field salad (also called lamb's lettuce)
  if available, or shredded lettuce or
  watercress

½ cup French or Vinaigrette Dressing
  (see page 155 for recipes)
Chopped hard-cooked eggs (garnish)

If using frozen asparagus, follow package instructions, cooking it a little less than instructed. If using fresh, scrape the stalks and remove tough ends. Steam the fresh asparagus for 10 to 15 minutes, depending upon the thickness of the stalks. It should be crisp-tender *not* mushy. Cool. Place on the greens. Pour the dressing over. Garnish with the chopped egg if you wish. Chill.

PARFAITS

(color plate 8)

Parfaits are easy to make. They must be layered into the glasses ahead, but they are very easy to serve. You do need space in the freezer to store them. Two kinds (2 colors) of ice cream or ice cream and sherbet give you the opportunity to vary color as well as taste and texture. It is also attractive to put a sauce in between layers. Use any combination you like—here are a few suggestions:

Chocolate ice cream and raspberry sherbet
Chocolate ice cream and lemon sherbet
Chocolate and coffee ice creams
Coffee ice cream and orange sherbet
Coffee ice cream and lime sherbet
Coffee and cherry or raspberry ice creams
Vanilla ice cream with almost any kind of ice cream or sherbet

Use your favorite sauces or fruit purees. Top, if you wish, with a dab of whipped cream.

COLD BUFFET

Vegetarian

Waldorf Salad
Avocado Aspic
Borscht Salad
Green Peppers Filled with Coleslaw
Deviled Eggs
Apricot Whole-Wheat Jelly Roll

WALDORF SALAD

⅓ cup Mayonnaise (see page 154 for recipe)
2 teaspoons lemon juice
Dash of salt

2 cups unpeeled, diced red apples
1½ to 2 cups diced celery
½ cup coarsely chopped walnuts
Lettuce leaves

In salad bowl blend mayonnaise, lemon juice and salt. Add apples, celery and walnuts and toss well. Serve on lettuce leaves.

AVOCADO ASPIC

1½ envelopes gelatin
1 cup cold water
1½ cups vegetable bouillon
1 teaspoon salt

1 tablespoon lemon juice
2 cloves garlic, crushed, or
  2 tablespoons grated onion
2 large or 4 medium-sized avocados

Soften the gelatin in water, and heat and stir to dissolve. Add the broth, salt, lemon juice and garlic. Peel the avocados, slice thin and add at once. Pour into a 1-quart mold and chill until firm.

BORSCHT SALAD

1 pound potatoes, cooked, peeled and
    diced
1 pound cabbage, shredded or diced
1 1-pound can diced beets, drained
    and juice reserved

1 onion, diced
1 tablespoon vinegar
1 teaspoon salt
1 cup sour cream

Combine the potatoes, cabbage and beets in a bowl. Stir 2 tablespoons of the reserved beet juice, onion, vinegar and salt into the sour cream. Spoon onto the salad and toss. Chill.

GREEN PEPPERS FILLED WITH COLESLAW

4 large green peppers
3 cups grated cabbage
1 large carrot, scraped and grated
1 large onion, grated
1 teaspoon salt
1 teaspoon sugar

½ teaspoon pepper
¼ cup oil
3 tablespoons vinegar
2 teaspoons caraway or poppy seeds
    (optional)

Cut the peppers in half and remove seeds. Combine the remaining ingredients and toss thoroughly. Pile into the pepper halves. You may use sweet red peppers instead of green.

DEVILED EGGS

8 hard-cooked eggs
1 teaspoon prepared mustard
2 teaspoons minced scallions or
    chives
3 tablespoons Mayonnaise (see page
    154 for recipe)

½ teaspoon *Fines Herbs* or marjoram
½ teaspoon curry powder (optional)
Parsley or paprika (garnish)

Cut the eggs in half and remove the yolks. Mash the yolks with a fork. Combine the remaining ingredients, mix well and add to the mashed yolks. Fill the egg whites with the mixture. Decorate the tops, if you wish, with a sprig of parsley or a dash of paprika.

APRICOT WHOLE-WHEAT JELLY ROLL

6 eggs
1¼ cups confectioners' sugar plus
    some for sprinkling on cake
⅓ cup whole-wheat flour

1½ teaspoons vanilla
Granulated sugar
¾ cup apricot preserves

Grease 15 x 10 x 1-inch jelly roll pan and line with waxed paper, extending paper a few inches at narrow ends. Grease paper, then set pan aside. In large bowl of mixer beat eggs at high speed until very light, about 5 minutes. Gradually add 1¼ cups confectioners' sugar, beating until very fluffy and lemon colored, about 5 minutes. Fold in flour and vanilla. Pour into greased pan and spread evenly. Bake at 350°F. for 20 to 25 minutes, or until pick inserted in center comes out clean. Cool in pan on rack for 5 minutes. Loosen edges with knife. Sprinkle a 15-inch length of waxed paper generously with granulated sugar, then invert cake onto paper. Carefully peel off waxed paper (baked with cake). If ragged, trim edges of cake. Starting at narrow end, roll up cake and fresh waxed paper as for a jelly roll. Cool on rack. Unroll, and spread evenly with preserves. Reroll *without* paper. Place seam side down, on dessert plate. Sift confectioners' sugar on roll. Cut in slices. Serves 8 to 10.

COLD BUFFET

Vegetarian

Spinach-Cheese Tart
Belgian Endive with Watercress
Vegetable Mold with Yogurt-Sesame Seed Dressing
Cracked Wheat and Peanut Loaf
Peppers Stuffed with Tomatoes
Rhubarb-Strawberry Bavarian
Shortbread Cookies

SPINACH-CHEESE TART

½ cup minced onion
2 tablespoons butter
¾ cup chopped cooked spinach
⅓ cup milk
1 teaspoon salt
¼ teaspoon pepper
4 eggs, slightly beaten

1 8-ounce package cream cheese, at
  room temperature
1 cup small-curd cottage cheese
Grated Parmesan cheese
9 or 10-inch baked pie shell
Strips of pimento or sweet red pepper
  (garnish)

Sauté the onion in butter only until transparent, not brown. Add to the spinach. Stir in the milk, salt and pepper and cook over low heat. Combine the eggs with the cheeses. Stir in the spinach mixture and pour into the pie shell. Decorate top with strips of pimento or red pepper. Bake at 350°F. for about 40 minutes, or until a pick inserted in center comes out clean. Serve at room temperature.

BELGIAN ENDIVE WITH WATERCRESS

8 small or 4 large heads Belgian
  endive
½ cup French Dressing (see page 155
  for recipe)

1 bunch watercress
12 to 18 nasturtiums (garnish)

Wash and trim the ends of the endive, if necessary. Separate a few of the large leaves and set aside. Cut the rest across in about ¼-inch slices. Put in a deep bowl and toss with half of the French Dressing. Line a salad bowl or deep platter with the reserved endive with the pointed ends out. Put some watercress between the endive around the edge, with the leaves out. The shades of green make an attractive border. Put the tossed endive in the center. Place the nasturtiums on the top of the salad and pour the remaining dressing over all. Nasturtium flowers are sweet, spicy and delicious. Toss at the buffet table.

VEGETABLE MOLD WITH YOGURT-SESAME SEED DRESSING

1 package lemon gelatin
1 cup boiling water
1 cup tomato or mixed vegetable juice
½ cup French Dressing (see page 155 for recipe)
1 small onion, minced

1 cup chopped celery
¼ cup chopped green pepper
½ cup chopped cucumber or zucchini
1 cup peeled, chopped fresh or canned Italian plum tomatoes
Greens (garnish)

Dissolve the gelatin in water. Add the juice. Chill until syrupy. Stir in the remaining ingredients. Pour into a 5-cup mold and chill until firm. Turn out on a cold serving plate and garnish with greens, if you wish. Serve the yogurt dressing on the side (recipe follows).

YOGURT-SESAME SEED DRESSING

⅔ cup plain yogurt
3 tablespoons toasted sesame seeds

2 tablespoons cider vinegar
2 tablespoons honey

Mix all the ingredients thoroughly. Use as dressing on greens or fruit. Yield: about 1 cup.

CRACKED WHEAT AND PEANUT LOAF

2 tablespoons oil
1 large onion, chopped
1½ cups cracked wheat (kasha)
2½ cups water
2 teaspoons salt

1 pound spinach
1½ cups unsalted peanuts
2 eggs
¼ teaspoon pepper

Heat oil in small saucepan and sauté onion and cracked wheat until onion is transparent. Add water and ½ teaspoon of the salt. Bring to boil, cover, reduce heat, and cook over very low heat until water is absorbed, about 15 minutes. Wash spinach and cook in only water that clings to the leaves in a covered pot until wilted, about five minutes. Place spinach, peanuts and eggs in blender or processor and process until creamed. Combine the spinach and cracked wheat mixtures. Mix thoroughly, adding the remaining 1½ teaspoons salt and pepper. Turn into an oiled loaf pan. Bake at 350°F. for about 1 hour. Chill until set. Serve at room temperature, cutting into slices.

PEPPERS STUFFED WITH TOMATOES

4 large green peppers
¾ teaspoon salt
3 cups chopped tomatoes
⅛ teaspoon pepper

¼ teaspoon sugar
¼ cup butter, melted
Buttered bread crumbs

Cut the peppers in half lengthwise, remove the seeds and membranes and parboil in water with ½ teaspoon of the salt for a minute or two. Drain the tomatoes of all their juice and combine with the remaining ingredients except bread crumbs. Fill the peppers with the tomatoes and top with crumbs. Bake at 375°F. for about 20 minutes, or until heated through and the crumbs are slightly browned.

RHUBARB-STRAWBERRY BAVARIAN

(color plate 8)

1 20-ounce package frozen cut
   rhubarb, partially thawed or 1½ to
   2 pounds fresh, trimmed and cut
   into 1-inch pieces (about 3 cups)
1 cup orange juice
1 3-ounce package strawberry flavor
   gelatin

⅔ cup heavy cream whipped with ¼
   cup sugar
Whipped cream and thin strips orange
   peel (optional)

In medium-sized saucepan over moderate heat, cook rhubarb in orange juice for 10 minutes, or until rhubarb is crisp-tender. Remove from heat and stir in gelatin until dissolved. Set pan in bowl of ice water and stir occasionally until mixture is cool. Fold in cream mixture. Turn into a serving bowl. Chill for several hours, or until firm. Garnish with whipped cream and orange peel, if you wish.

SHORTBREAD COOKIES

2 hard-cooked egg yolks
¼ cup sugar
½ cup butter

1 cup flour
½ teaspoon almond extract
Superfine sugar

Sieve the egg yolks and combine with the sugar. Cream the butter, add the egg yolks-sugar and beat until light and fluffy. Stir in the flour and almond extract. Chill. Form into small flattened balls, about ¾ inch in diameter, and bake on a baking sheet for 10 minutes at 375°F. Sprinkle with superfine sugar while still hot. Yield: about 25 cookies.

Plate 1
Beef Salad with Tomatoes,
Prosciutto and Lettuce Salad,
Salmon Salad

Plate 2

**Roast Loin of Pork, Spareribs,
Ham Ring**

Plate 3
Fried Rice, Sweet and Sour Chicken,
Crab-Pork-Pepper Wedges,
Steak Kew with Broccoli, Tea Eggs,
Wonton Soup,
Shrimp Pork Egg Rolls, Almond Cookies

 Plate 4

Platter of Marinated Vegetables,
Garden Vegetable Soup,
Eggplant with Tomato Slices

Plate 5

Italian Three-Bean Salad with Tuna,
Beef and Broccoli,
Noodle Salad with Ham

Plate 8
Rhubarb-Strawberry Bavarian,
Parfaits, Baked Alaska

COLD BUFFET

Grapefruit
Boeuf à la Mode
Chicken with Ginger
Garlic French Bread
Tomatoes Stuffed with Egg Salad
Zabaglione

BOEUF À LA MODE

1 4½ pound piece of boned rump, or
   round of beef
1½ cups red wine
1 teaspoon salt
¼ teaspoon pepper
1 onion, sliced

1 bay leaf, crumbled
¼ cup shortening
2 cups beef broth
2 envelopes gelatin
¼ cup sherry

Have the meat tied into a roll, if necessary. Place in a large bowl with the wine, salt, pepper, onion and bay leaf and marinate for at least 12 hours, turning several times. Remove from marinade and pat dry. Save the marinade. Brown the beef on all sides in the shortening, taking about 20 minutes. Pour in the marinade and 1 cup of the beef broth. If there is not enough liquid, add more wine or broth. Cover tightly and simmer for about 3 hours, or until tender. Turn the meat 3 or 4 times. Cool and trim off any fat. Chill overnight. Soften the gelatin in ½ cup of the broth and add to the marinade with the remaining ½ cup broth and the sherry. Heat and stir until the gelatin is dissolved. You'll need about 4 cups of liquid. Add wine, broth or water, if needed. Chill until syrupy. Slice the meat thin on a large platter and pour two-thirds of the syrupy aspic over. Chill until set. Pour the remaining aspic over. If it has set, you will have to heat it slightly over warm water. Chill again for several hours until set. Serves 10 to 12.

CHICKEN WITH GINGER

Substitute ½ cup chicken broth for half the cream in Chicken with Wine (see page 100 for recipe) and add 1 teaspoon grated fresh ginger root to the sauce. Pour a little sauce over the chicken and serve the rest on the side.

TOMATOES STUFFED WITH EGG SALAD

8 medium-sized ripe tomatoes
4 hard-cooked eggs, chopped
¾ cup Mayonnaise (see page 154 for recipe)
2 teaspoons prepared mustard
2 tablespoons minced onion

½ teaspoon salt
¼ teaspoon pepper
½ teaspoon sugar
1 tablespoon chopped fresh thyme or 3 tablespoons minced parsley (optional)

Cut a slice from the top of the unpeeled tomatoes and scoop out the flesh. Combine the eggs with half of the tomato flesh and the remaining ingredients. If too thick, add a little of the juice from the tomatoes. Refill the tomatoes and chill. You may top with a little of the thyme or minced parsley, if you wish.

ZABAGLIONE

6 egg yolks
⅔ cup superfine sugar

⅔ cup Marsala or sweet sherry

Beat the egg yolks in a bowl with a rotary beater until light colored. Gradually add the sugar while continuing to beat. Transfer to a double boiler and beat over simmering water about 7 minutes until the mixture foams up and becomes quite thick. Then gradually beat in the Marsala or sherry. Do not overcook. Do not let the water in the bottom of the double boiler touch the upper pan. Serve at room temperature or chill.

COLD BUFFET

Hearts of Palm
Fish Fillets with Dill Mayonnaise
Steamed Chicken with Wine
Italian Three-Bean Salad with Tuna
Spiced Zucchini
Genoa Toast (or Italian Breadsticks)
Caramel Custard
Chocolate Cookies

HEARTS OF PALM

2 14-ounce cans hearts of palm
½ cup French Dressing made with
    white vinegar (see page 155 for
    recipe)

1 tablespoon chopped fresh tarragon,
    dill and/or chives
1 tablespoon minced parsley

Drain the hearts and cut large ones in half lengthwise. Divide the salad among 8 salad plates or put on a platter, placing the cut sides down. Combine the dressing with the herbs. Mix thoroughly and pour over. Chill for several hours.

FISH FILLETS WITH DILL MAYONNAISE

3 pounds thick fish fillets (cod,
    flounder, sole, turbot, sea bass
    or lake trout)
2 tablespoons white wine
½ teaspoon salt
1½ tablespoons minced fresh dill, or 1
    teaspoon dried

1 cup Mayonnaise* or Mayonnaise
    made with Lemon (see page 154 for
    recipe)
Lemon wedges
Sprigs of fresh dill (garnish)

*See Index

Place the fish on a sheet of foil, add wine and salt. Fold the foil over carefully and bake at 400° F. for 20 to 25 minutes. Cool. Remove the fish to a cold platter. Handle the fish carefully; fillets break easily. Chill. Add the dill and the liquid from the fish to the mayonnaise. Spoon a thin layer over each fillet. Serve with lemon wedges and decorate with sprigs of dill, if available.

STEAMED FISH STICKS

Substitute fish cut into sticks (halibut, cod or swordfish) for the fillets and proceed as for Fish Fillets with Dill Mayonnaise. (recipe precedes)

STEAMED CHICKEN WITH WINE

1 4½ pound chicken	2 egg yolks, slightly beaten
1½ teaspoons salt	¼ teaspoon white pepper
¼ cup white wine	Parsley, pimento or watercress
1 cup cream	(garnish)

Rub the chicken with 1 teaspoon of the salt and place it on a large piece of foil. Add 2 tablespoons of the wine and close the foil. Bake at 375° F. for 1½ hours. Remove and cool. Pour off the liquid. Chill in the freezer compartment for 1 hour. Remove the skin from the chicken on a platter. Heat the cream adding about ½ cup of defatted juice from the chicken. Add remaining wine, stir in the egg yolks, remaining ½ teaspoon salt and the pepper. Cook until slightly thickened. Cool. Adjust seasoning and pour over the chicken. Chill for a number of hours. Garnish, if you wish.

ITALIAN THREE-BEAN SALAD WITH TUNA

(color plate 5)

1 16-ounce can kidney beans	1 large green pepper, cut into rings
1 16-ounce can chick-peas, drained	2 pimentos, cut in strips
1 10-ounce package frozen cut green beans, cooked and chilled	16 large pitted ripe olives, left whole
¾ cup Italian dressing	2 7-ounce cans tuna
Lettuce leaves	

In a large bowl combine the beans and pour ½ cup of the dressing over. Line a platter with lettuce leaves. Make a mound in the center with the tuna and surround with the bean salad. Top with green pepper rings, pimento and olives. Pour the remaining dressing over. Chill.

SPICED ZUCCHINI

6 medium-sized zucchini, sliced
½ inch thick
¼ cup butter
2 tablespoons oil

2 large tomatoes, peeled and chopped
½ teaspoon curry or chili powder
1 teaspoon salt
¼ teaspoon pepper

In large skillet sauté zucchini in butter and oil for 5 minutes, or until golden, turning slices once. Add tomato and seasonings. Bring to boil, reduce heat, cover and simmer for about 5 minutes.

CARAMEL CUSTARD

Caramel Sauce:

1 cup sugar

½ cup water

Brown the sugar. Add the water. Stir and simmer for 5 minutes until the caramel dissolves. Cool slightly and pour into custard cups or mold. Swish around to coat the sides. When the caramel is firm, pour in the custard (see recipe below) and proceed as directed.

Baked Custard:

4 eggs
⅓ cup sugar
Salt

3 cups milk
1 teaspoon vanilla

Beat the eggs until blended; stir in sugar and salt. Heat the milk; pour slowly on the eggs while stirring. Add vanilla. Pour custard into custard cups or mold that have been coated with caramel sauce (see preceding recipe). Place custard cups in a pan of water, the cups resting on a rack but also touching the water, and bake at 350°F. for about 40 minutes. Cool and unmold to serve.

CHOCOLATE COOKIES

2 ounces unsweetened chocolate
½ cup melted butter
½ teaspoon salt
1 cup sugar

½ cup flour
2 eggs, well beaten
1 teaspoon vanilla
½ cup finely chopped walnuts

Melt the chocolate in a double boiler. Remove from the heat and add the butter, salt, sugar and flour. Beat well. Then add the eggs and vanilla. Beat thoroughly. With a spatula spread the batter as thin as you possibly can on a greased baking sheet. Sprinkle with the walnuts. Bake at 400°F. for 10 minutes. Cut into squares while the cookies are still warm because they get crisp very quickly. Yield: about 3 dozen.

COLD BUFFET

Pâté Maison
Toast or Rye Rounds
Vitello Tonnato
Avocado Halves with Lemon French Dressing
Salmon Salad
Green Bean Salad
Apple Pie

PÂTÉ MAISON

1 pound pork, cut up
1 pound veal, cut up
½ pound pork, beef or calves' liver,
    cut up
1 small onion or 2 shallots, cut up

2 tablespoons chopped parsley
1 teaspoon salt
¼ teaspoon pepper
½ teaspoon ground ginger (optional)
1 tablespoon brandy or rum (optional)

Combine all of the ingredients and puree in a blender or processor. Spoon into a buttered loaf pan. Cover and bake at 375°F. for 1 hour. Cool and then chill for about 24 hours. Turn out or serve from the pan.

VITELLO TONNATO

3 pounds rolled veal roast (or boned
    piece)
1 bay leaf
1 stalk celery, cut up
1 carrot, scraped and cut up
4 sprigs parsley
1 small onion, cut up

1 teaspoon salt
2 7-ounce cans tuna
1 2-ounce can anchovies
2 tablespoons lemon juice
½ cup olive oil
2 tablespoons capers

Put the veal in a large pot with the bay leaf, celery, carrot, parsley, onion, salt and water partly to cover. Cover tightly and steam until the veal is tender, about 1½ hours. Make the sauce by pureeing the tuna, anchovies and lemon juice in a blender or food processor. Pour in the oil very slowly; it should thicken. Add the capers and 2 or 3 tablespoons pureed vegetables from the pot the veal was cooked in. When the veal is cool, slice it thin and place in slightly overlapping slices on a chilled deep platter. Pour the tuna sauce over. Chill overnight.

AVOCADO HALVES WITH LEMON FRENCH DRESSING

6 medium to large avocados
Juice of 1 lemon

½ cup Lemon French Dressing (see page 155 for recipe)
Lettuce

Cut the avocados in half and remove the pits. Sprinkle the edges with lemon juice to prevent discoloration. Fill the centers with dressing and serve on a bed of lettuce. Serves 12.

SALMON SALAD

(color plate 1)

1 bunch watercress
2 15½-ounce cans salmon
2 large onions, chopped fine

½ cup white-wine vinegar
2 tablespoons oil
½ teaspoon pepper

Remove tough stems from watercress and break into sprigs. Drain the salmon, reserving liquid, and break into large chunks. Arrange watercress on a platter, then add salmon and onion, leaving a border of cress. Combine the liquid from the salmon with vinegar. Add oil and pepper, then taste for seasoning; you may need more pepper. Pour over the salad.

GREEN BEAN SALAD

1½ to 2 pounds young tender green beans
⅓ cup oil (part or all olive)
¼ cup wine vinegar
1 teaspoon salt

¼ teaspoon pepper
½ teaspoon sugar
2 tablespoons chopped fresh summer savory or 2 teaspoons dried
3 tablespoons chopped or slivered almonds, or sesame seeds

Cut the ends from the beans and put them in 2 or 3 bunches all in one direction. Boil for about 6 minutes in salted water. Drain and rinse at once in cold water. Chill. You may use larger beans, cut French-style. Make the dressing by combining the remaining ingredients, except almonds. If summer savory is not available, and you have other fresh herbs, substitute one such as basil, oregano or chervil. If not, use the dried summer savory. Pour over the beans and chill again. Sprinkle with almonds or sesame seeds.

APPLE PIE

2 9-inch 2-layer pie crusts (4 crusts
   for 2 pies)
6–8 cups sliced peeled tart cooking
   apples (about 2½ pounds)
½ cup sugar
¼ cup light-brown sugar, packed
2 tablespoons flour

¼ teaspoon salt
⅛ teaspoon nutmeg
⅛ teaspoon grated lemon peel
2 teaspoons sherry or lemon juice
2 tablespoons butter
Pieces of Cheddar cheese (optional)

Line two 9-inch pie pans with pastry. Mix the ingredients except butter and fill pie shell. Dot with the butter. Roll out top crusts and cut slits in several places for steam to escape. Moisten edges of crusts well with cold water and adjust top crusts. With fingers or fork, pinch two crusts together to make tight seals around pies. Bake at 400°F. for 15 minutes. Reduce heat to 350°F. and bake about 45 minutes longer. Serve warm or at room temperature, with pieces of cheese on the side.

COLD BUFFET

Mussels with Tomato Sauce
Smoked Tongue
Mackenzie Chicken Salad
Watercress Salad with Cherry Tomatoes
Greek Rice Salad
Meringue Shell Filled with Cut-up Fresh Fruit

MUSSELS WITH TOMATO SAUCE

6 dozen medium to large mussels
2 cloves garlic, or 2 onions, minced
½ cup tomato sauce or tomato puree

1 teaspoon Worcestershire sauce
½ teaspoon sugar
½ teaspoon pepper

Cut beards from mussels and place in pot with 1 cup water. Cover tight and steam until the mussels open, about 3 or 4 minutes. Chill the mussels and pull off the top shells. Place 9 on each of 8 plates. Combine the remaining ingredients and mix well. Adjust the seasoning and spoon over the mussels.

SMOKED TONGUE

1 4-pound smoked tongue
1 onion, cut up
1 stalk celery, cut up
1 bay leaf

½ teaspoon pepper
Mustard, Horseradish or Raisin
    Sauces (optional)

Put the tongue in a large pot with water to cover and add all of the ingredients except the sauces. Cover and boil for about 3 hours, adding more water, if needed. When cool enough to handle, peel and cut away any small bones and gristle. Return to the pot and cook until tender, about 30 minutes. Let the tongue cool in its broth. Remove from the broth and place on a cold platter. Carve at the table or slice thin. Pass the sauce of your choice.

MACKENZIE CHICKEN SALAD

1 6- to 7-pound roasting chicken
4 stalks celery
1 cup Mayonnaise (see page 154 for
   recipe)
½ cup sour cream

1 tablespoon curry powder
2 tablespoons chutney
Salt and pepper (optional)
Shredded lettuce or watercress

Roast the chicken at 375°F. for about 1½ hours. Cover with foil for the last 30 minutes of cooking or cook, wrapped in foil, in a preheated oven. Scrape the celery and cut into large dice. As soon as the chicken is cool enough to handle, pull the skin off and cut the meat into bite-sized pieces. Pour the juices into a cup and refrigerate. When ready to put the salad together, combine the mayonnaise with sour cream and curry. If the chutney is in large pieces, either cut up in a blender or processor or mince it fine. Stir into the mayonnaise. Add a little defatted juice from the chicken. If the juice is too firm, heat it slightly and stir in. Taste for seasoning. You will probably need salt, pepper and possibly more curry. Fold the dressing into the salad. Chill. Serve on shredded lettuce or watercress.

WATERCRESS SALAD WITH CHERRY TOMATOES

2 bunches watercress
2 boxes cherry tomatoes, hulled

3 tablespoons minced chives or
   scallions
⅓ cup French Dressing (see page 155
   for recipe)

Remove the heavy stems from the watercress and chop the leaves. Put into a bowl with the tomatoes. Add the chives or scallions and half the dressing. Chill for a few hours. Pour the remaining dressing over and toss.

GREEK RICE SALAD

(color plate 6, top)

4 cups cooked rice, chilled
3 tablespoons olive oil
3 tablespoons lemon juice
1 teaspoon salt
¼ teaspoon pepper
1 tablespoon chopped chives
1 tablespoon parsley

¾ teaspoon dill
¾ cup peeled, seeded and chopped
   cucumber
½ cup peeled, seeded and chopped
   tomato
Avocado and tomato slices and
   spinach leaves for garnish (optional)

In large bowl mix well rice, oil, lemon juice, salt, pepper, chives, parsley and dill. Fold in cucumber and tomato. Chill well. If desired, salad can be turned into ring mold, chilled and turned out on a platter. Fill center with avocado and tomato slices and spinach or other green leaves.

MERINGUE SHELL

4 egg whites, at room temperature
¼ teaspoon salt
½ teaspoon cream of tartar

1 cup sugar, preferably superfine
½ teaspoon vanilla

Lightly grease 10-inch wide 1½-inch deep pie plate. Beat egg whites and salt until foamy. Beat in cream of tartar. Continue beating while gradually adding sugar, 2 tablespoons at a time, beating well after each addition until sugar dissolves and meringue is very stiff and glossy but not dry. Beat in vanilla. Spread a 1-inch layer of meringue on bottom of pie plate. Spread remaining meringue around sides, building it up about ½ inch higher than plate rim. Smooth lightly with spatula dipped in water. Bake at 250°F. for 1 hour. Turn off oven and let shell dry in closed oven until cool. Then fill with fresh cut-up fruit of your choice.

COLD BUFFET

Sengalese Soup
Chicken Potato Salad
Halibut in Marinade
Melba Toast
Beef Salad with Tomatoes
Celery-Mushroom Salad
Lemon Yellow Cake with Lemon Butter-Cream Icing

SENGALESE SOUP

4 onions, chopped
2 apples, peeled, cored and cut up
3 tablespoons butter
1 teaspoon curry powder
¼ cup flour

1 teaspoon salt
1 quart chicken broth
2 cups half-and-half
Chopped parsley or minced chicken
  (garnish)

Sauté the onion and apple in butter until onion is transparent but not brown. Stir in the curry powder, flour and salt until smooth. Pour in the broth slowly while stirring. Cook until slightly thickened. Put into a processor or blender and puree. It will take only a minute. Chill and stir in half-and-half. Top with parsley and/or minced chicken, if you wish.

CHICKEN POTATO SALAD

3 large chicken breasts, cooked
1 pound small potatoes, boiled and
    peeled
¼ cup Mayonnaise (see page 154 for
    recipe)

1 tablespoon lemon juice
¼ teaspoon pepper
Salt
½ cup sliced olives

Remove the skin and bones from the chicken and cut into ½ x 2-inch strips. Cut the potatoes into strips about the same size as the chicken. Blend the mayonnaise with the lemon juice and pepper. Add salt to taste. Combine the chicken, potatoes and olives. Spoon the dressing over and toss gently. Chill.

HALIBUT IN MARINADE

8 pieces halibut (about ⅓ pound each)
¼ cup oil (olive or part vegetable)
2 tablespoons lemon juice
1 teaspoon salt

¼ teaspoon pepper
1 tablespoon chopped parsley
Chopped dill, thyme or parsley

Place the fish in a dish. Combine the oil, lemon juice, salt and pepper and pour over the fish. Refrigerate for several hours, turning to ensure all sides being covered with the marinade. Drain, saving the marinade. Broil the fish about 10 minutes, turn and broil 5 minutes more. Return the fish to the marinade and chill. Serve with a little of the liquid poured over the fish. Sprinkle with the herbs.

BEEF SALAD WITH TOMATOES

(color plate 1)

2½ pounds cooked beef, cut into
    cubes
½ cup minced parsley
⅓ cup minced scallions
3 tablespoons wine vinegar
⅓ cup olive oil
1 teaspoon salt
¼ teaspoon pepper

1 head Boston lettuce
4 hard-cooked eggs, cut in half
6 large tomatoes, peeled and cut in
    wedges
Mayonnaise (see page 154 for recipe)
2 teaspoons fresh tarragon or
    1 teaspoon dried
2 tablespoons chopped chives

Mix the beef with parsley and scallions. Combine the vinegar, oil, salt and pepper and pour over the beef. Line a platter with lettuce leaves and pile beef in middle. Place the eggs and tomatoes around the edge of the platter. Top the eggs with a dab of mayonnaise and sprinkle tarragon and chives over all.

CELERY-MUSHROOM SALAD

1 head celery	1 teaspoon salt
1 pound mushrooms	¼ teaspoon pepper
½ cup olive oil	Bibb or other lettuce (optional)
2 tablespoons lemon juice	

Pull the celery apart, wash and scrape the stalks. Cut across into slices not over ¼ inch thick. Wipe the mushrooms and remove the stems completely by pulling or popping them out, but not by merely cutting them off. Cut the mushrooms across the heads in slices about the thickness of the celery. They will make half moon slices similar to the celery. Put together in a bowl and toss. Mix the oil, lemon juice, salt and pepper and pour over the mushrooms. This salad may be completely made at least 1 hour before dinner. It improves by standing in the dressing. If you wish, you may serve it on salad greens.

LEMON YELLOW CAKE

½ cup butter	1¾ cups cake flour
1 cup sugar	½ teaspoon salt
2 eggs, well beaten	2½ teaspoons baking powder
2 tablespoons lemon juice	½ cup milk
2½ teaspoons grated lemon peel	

Cream the butter and gradually add the sugar. Cream until light and fluffy. Add the eggs, lemon juice and peel. Mix well. Sift the flour, salt and baking powder together. Add to the butter-sugar mixture alternately with the milk. Pour into 2 8-inch layer cake pans 1½ inches deep and lined with waxed paper. Bake at 375°F. for 20 to 25 minutes. Turn out on racks, remove paper and cool before frosting (recipe follows). Serves 8 to 10.

LEMON BUTTER-CREAM ICING

¼ cup butter	3 to 4 tablespoons half-and-half or
3 cups confectioners' sugar, sifted	milk
1 egg yolk	1 teaspoon lemon extract

Cream the butter with sugar, adding the sugar gradually. When about half the sugar has been added, add the egg yolk and beat thoroughly until the mixture is fluffy. Add the rest of the sugar alternately with the half-and-half or milk. Use only enough liquid to reach a proper spreading consistency. Flavor with the lemon extract. Yield: enough for a 9-inch 2-layer cake.

COLD BUFFET

Melba Toast
Salmon in Aspic
Green Sauce
Macaroni-Beef Salad
Cucumbers with Yogurt
Raw Vegetable Salad
Macedoine of Fresh Fruit
Butterscotch Brownies

SALMON IN ASPIC

1 6-pound salmon	2 tablespoons butter
1 teaspoon salt	1 envelope gelatin
½ teaspoon pepper	¾ cup white wine
½ teaspoon thyme	1 egg white, slightly beaten
2 bay leaves	Decorative garnishes
¼ cup chopped celery	

Place the salmon, with head and tail left on, on a large piece of foil or two pieces of cheesecloth. Put on the rack of a long fish steamer. Pour in about 1 quart of water with the salt, pepper, thyme, bay leaves and celery. Cover tightly and steam for 40 minutes. If you do not have a steamer long enough to hold the fish, which must lie flat, you can steam it in foil. Fold into a large piece of foil with the salt, pepper, thyme and butter. Fold tight so that no liquid can escape and bake at 400°F. for 45 minutes. In either case let the fish rest for 20 minutes. Lift out, open the foil or cheesecloth. Pull and scrape the skin off the fish. It is easy to do while the fish is warm. Roll out onto a platter and remove skin from the other side. Soften the gelatin in ½ cup liquid from the steamer or juices from the foil, adding a little wine to make ½ cup. Add remaining wine and heat to dissolve the gelatin. Remove from heat and stir in the egg white. This clears the aspic. Cool until syrupy and spoon into a thin layer over the fish. Chill until the aspic is set. Decorate the salmon in any way you like, using sliced stuffed olives, sliced carrots, green pepper slivers, lemon slices, leaves of watercress, small sprigs of dill or parsley. Design a pretty picture! Cover with the remaining aspic. If it has become too stiff, warm it slightly. Decorate the platter with lemon wedges and greens. This is an expensive, impressive dish and should look its best for a festive occasion. Serve Green Sauce (recipe follows) and/or mayonnaise on the buffet. Serves 10.

GREEN SAUCE

½ cup minced spinach
2 tablespoons parsley
2 tablespoons minced chives
2 tablespoons water

1 cup Mayonnaise (see page 154 for recipe)
Food coloring (optional)

Put the spinach, parsley and chives in a small pot with the water and simmer, covered, for 2 or 3 minutes. Puree by forcing through a sieve or in a blender or processor. Mix into the mayonnaise. This is the best way to make a green colored sauce. However, you may add the vegetables raw, but be sure they are minced very fine. If you want the sauce to look really green, add a drop or two of food coloring. Yield: about 1½ cups.

MACARONI-BEEF SALAD

1 pound small-shell macaroni
1½ teaspoons salt
½ cup Mayonnaise (see page 154 for recipe)
¼ teaspoon pepper
2 tablespoons oil

1 tablespoon vinegar
1 cup diced celery
4 scallions, chopped
3 cups diced cooked beef
Lettuce

Cook the macaroni according to package instructions, using 1 teaspoon of the salt. Do not overcook. Drain. Mix the mayonnaise with pepper, oil, vinegar and remaining ½ teaspoon salt. Spoon over the macaroni, toss and add the celery, scallions and beef. Stir thoroughly and chill. Serve in lettuce cups or on shredded lettuce.

CUCUMBERS WITH YOGURT

6 slender cucumbers
1 teaspoon salt
1 cup yogurt
1½ teaspoons vinegar flavored with 1 clove garlic, crushed (let garlic stand in vinegar for 1 hour, then discard)

½ teaspoon dried dill or 1 tablespoon fresh chopped
1 tablespoon minced fresh mint leaves

Peel cucumbers. Slice very thin by hand or in a processor. Put in a bowl and sprinkle generously with salt to draw out bitter juices. Refrigerate for several hours or overnight. Drain and rinse thoroughly. Mix yogurt, vinegar and dill until smooth and combine with cucumbers. Serve chilled, sprinkled with mint.

RAW VEGETABLE SALAD

2 cups thinly sliced carrots
1 cup thinly sliced celery
2 cups thinly sliced cucumbers
½ cup thinly sliced sweet red peppers
½ cup chopped red onion
½ cup cauliflower or broccoli
  flowerets
⅓ cup oil

¼ cup vinegar (scant)
1 teaspoon salt
¼ teaspoon pepper
2 teaspoons sugar
½ teaspoon curry powder
½ teaspoon dried tarragon, thyme or
  basil

Mix the vegetables in a bowl. Combine the remaining ingredients in a jar, cover and shake well. Pour over the vegetables and refrigerate for several hours. Serve in a deep plate or shallow bowl. Serves 8 to 10.

MACEDOINE OF FRUITS

1 quart strawberries
1 large pineapple peeled and cut into
  bite-sized pieces
4 large oranges, peeled and sectioned
6 peaches, peeled and sliced

1 quart blackberries or black
  raspberries, if available
½ cup superfine sugar
½ cup kirsch, Cointreau, rum,
  Madeira or brandy

Mix the fruits together and add the sugar and spirits. Serves 10 to 12.

BUTTERSCOTCH BROWNIES

½ cup flour
⅛ teaspoon salt
1 teaspoon baking powder
¼ cup butter

1 cup brown sugar
1 egg
1 teaspoon vanilla
½ cup finely chopped nuts

Sift the flour, salt and baking powder together. Melt the butter and stir in the sugar. Continue stirring until dissolved. Cool slightly before beating in the egg and vanilla. Blend in the flour mixture. Add the nuts and pour into a greased 8 x 8 x 2-inch pan. Bake at 350°F. for 30 minutes. Cut into 1 x 2-inch bars. Yield: 32 brownies.

IV

FORK-FOOD BUFFETS

For a very large crowd, there may be no way for all the guests to have a table to sit at. This means you cannot use a knife. The food needs no apology; it can be delicious. There are casseroles, stews with a European background, kabobs, which are always made of bite-sized pieces and can be pushed off the skewers onto the dinner plate. Meal salads can contain combinations of small pastas, rice, potatoes and meat, fish or vegetables. Shellfish and fish can be managed with one hand and so, of course, can most vegetables and dinner salads. Many desserts fit into the fork-food category. (Recipes are for 10 or more.)

FORK-FOOD

Vegetarian

Bean-Peanut Stew
Mushroom Kabobs
Salad Niçoise
Cheese Tray with Crackers
Rice with Lemon
Five-Bean Salad
Pineapple and Strawberries
Whole-Wheat Date Bars

BEAN-PEANUT STEW

2½ cups dried pea (navy) beans, rinsed and picked over
2 large onions, chopped
2 medium-sized green peppers, seeded and chopped
3 tablespoons butter or margarine
2 cups thinly sliced carrots
2 cups dried black-eyed peas, rinsed and picked over

¼ teaspoon crushed red pepper
6 cups water
1½ cups peanut butter
1 teaspoon salt
2 teaspoons chopped coriander or Italian parsley
1 teaspoon basil
3 tablespoons chopped fresh parsley for garnish (optional)

In medium saucepan cover pea beans with water and soak overnight or bring to boil, cook for 2 minutes, remove from heat and let stand, covered, for 1 hour; drain. In Dutch oven or large heavy pot sauté onion and green pepper in butter or margarine until onion is golden. Add carrots, pea beans, péas, red pepper and water, bring to boil and stir. Reduce heat, cover and, stirring occasionally and adding water if needed, simmer 1½ to 2 hours, or until beans are tender. In medium bowl stir peanut butter, 1 cup hot broth from pot, salt, coriander or Italian parsley and basil until smooth. Stir into pot. Cover and simmer for 15 minutes to blend seasonings. Serve sprinkled with parsley. Serves 10.

MUSHROOM KABOBS

2½ to 3 pounds medium to large
    mushrooms
½ cup melted butter

1½ teaspoons salt
½ teaspoon oregano
Minced chives (optional)

Trim the mushroom stems and wipe the mushrooms. Parboil for 1 minute; this prevents their splitting when you put them on the skewers. Thread on 12 skewers, brush with butter and sprinkle with salt and oregano. Broil for 4 minutes, turn and broil for 2 minutes more. Sprinkle with chives, if you wish. Serves 12.

SALAD NIÇOISE

6 small new potatoes
1 cup French Dressing (see page 155
    for recipe)
3 cups cut fresh green beans or 2
    10-ounce packages frozen
½ cup seeded, chopped green pepper
1 large red onion, sliced thin and
    separated into rings

1 2-ounce can anchovies
1 6½-ounce can tuna
3 medium-sized tomatoes, peeled and
    quartered
3 hard-cooked eggs, quartered
18 pitted black olives

Cook the potatoes in their skins until just tender; be careful not to overcook them. Peel and dice while warm and pour ¼ cup of the French Dressing over. Refrigerate. Cook the beans until crisp-tender. If using frozen beans, follow package instructions, cooking a couple of minutes less than suggested. Drain the beans and combine with the green pepper, onion and anchovies. Add 3 tablespoons dressing and refrigerate. When ready to assemble the salad, pile the potatoes in the center of a platter and surround with the bean mixture. Garnish with pieces of tuna, the tomatoes, eggs and olives. Pour the remaining dressing over. Toss at the buffet.

RICE WITH LEMON

5 cups water
3 teaspoons lemon juice
3 tablespoons butter

1 teaspoon salt
2½ cups rice

In heavy saucepan bring water, lemon juice, butter and salt to a rapid boil. Add rice, cover and cook over low heat about 20 minutes until rice is tender and water absorbed. Serves 10 to 12.

FIVE-BEAN SALAD

1 10-ounce package cut green beans
1 10-ounce package cut wax beans
1 10-ounce package small lima beans
1 8-ounce can kidney beans, drained
1 8-ounce can garbanzos, drained

1 large onion, diced
1 cup French Dressing (see page 155 for recipe)
1 teaspoon prepared mustard

Cook the frozen vegetables according to package instructions, being sure not to overcook. Drain and chill. Combine with the canned beans and onion. Toss to blend thoroughly. Mix the mustard with the French Dressing. Pour over the salad and chill a number of hours or overnight. Serves 10 to 12.

PINEAPPLE AND STRAWBERRIES

2 fresh pineapples, or 2 20-ounce cans
5 pints strawberries, hulled and sliced

¼ cup honey, warmed
¼ cup brandy

Peel the pineapple, cut into quarters, core and slice thin. If using canned pineapple, drain. Put the berries into the center of a deep serving plate or shallow bowl, preferably glass, and surround with pineapple. Stir the honey into the brandy. (If using canned pineapple, add 3 tablespoons juice.) Blend well. Pour over the fruit. Chill for several hours. Serves 12.

WHOLE-WHEAT DATE BARS

1¼ cups water
1 8-ounce package pitted dates, chopped
1⅔ cups whole-wheat flour
1 cup wheat germ
1 cup brown sugar

½ cup butter, softened
1 teaspoon baking powder
½ teaspoon salt
2 eggs
¼ teaspoon almond extract

In saucepan bring to boil water and dates. Reduce heat and simmer, uncovered, for 15 to 20 minutes or until dates thicken and water is absorbed. Mix well 1 cup of the whole-wheat flour, the wheat germ, ½ cup of the sugar and the butter. Work with hands until mixture resembles coarse crumbs. Press 2 cups mixture into 9 × 9 × 2-inch baking pan and set remainder aside. Bake crust at 350°F. for 10 minutes. Meanwhile, blend date mixture, remaining ⅔ cup whole-wheat flour, remaining ½ cup sugar, the baking powder, salt, eggs and almond extract. Spread evenly over baked crust. Sprinkle with reserved wheat-germ mixture, pressing in lightly. Bake at 350°F. for 25 minutes. Cool in pan on rack. Cut into 2¼ × 1-inch bars. Yield: about 3 dozen bars.

FORK-FOOD

Baked Stuffed Mushrooms
Pork Kabobs
Steak and Kidney Pie
Golden Risotto
Succotash
Avocados Stuffed with Cream Cheese or Roquefort
Herb Marinated Nectarines
White Layer Cake with Delicious Chocolate Frosting

BAKED STUFFED MUSHROOMS

2 pounds medium-sized mushrooms
1 cup chopped pecans
6 tablespoons chopped parsley
½ cup soft butter
1 clove garlic, crushed

½ teaspoon oregano
1 teaspoon salt
Dash of pepper
¾ cup cream

Wipe the mushrooms with a damp cloth. Remove the caps and arrange in a shallow baking dish, hollow side up. Chop the stems and mix with the remaining ingredients, except the cream. Heap the filling into the mushroom caps and press down firmly. Pour the cream over, cover and bake at 350°F. for 30 minutes, or until tender. Baste once or twice with the cream in the dish, adding a little more if necessary. Serves 10 to 12 as a canapé; 8 as a main dish.

PORK KABOBS

4 pounds lean pork from leg, cut into
   ¾-inch cubes
¾ cup soy sauce
¼ cup sherry
1 teaspoon prepared mustard
1 teaspoon sugar
1 tablespoon minced onion

¼ teaspoon sage
24 to 30 boiling onions
2 large or 3 medium-sized green
   peppers, cut into 1-inch pieces
12 crab apples, cut in half, or 6 large
   firm apples, quartered

Marinate the pork for several hours in a mixture of the soy sauce, sherry, mustard, sugar, minced onion and sage. Thread on 12 skewers, alternating the pork with onions, peppers and apples. Broil slowly under a broiler, turning once. The cooking time will be about 20 minutes. Do not use apples that are too ripe or they will fall off the skewers. Each person can push the pork off the skewers onto his plate, if the meal is to be eaten without a table to sit at. Serves 12.

STEAK AND KIDNEY PIE

2 to 2½ pounds lean beef, cut into 1-inch cubes	½ cup flour
½ teaspoon meat tenderizer	2 teaspoons salt
Pastry for 2-crust pie	¼ teaspoon pepper
4 veal, 8 lamb, or 1 to 2 beef kidneys	3 tablespoons melted butter
3 cups broth	1 clove garlic, crushed
	Pinch of savory

Sprinkle the beef with the meat tenderizer, piercing the meat with a fork, and let stand at room temperature for 30 minutes. Roll out the bottom crust, line the pie plate and store in the refrigerator until needed. Meanwhile, remove the fat from the kidneys; if using beef, cover with the broth and simmer for 16 minutes. Remove, cut into thin slices and trim off any fat and membranes. Dredge the beef with ¼ cup of the flour, seasoned with half the salt and pepper. Brown in the melted butter. Add the garlic, kidneys and remaining flour. Heat and stir until the flour turns golden. Pour in the broth and season with the savory and remaining salt and pepper. Cover and simmer for about 30 minutes, or until the meat is almost tender. Pour into the crust, cover with the top crust and make slits for steam. Bake for 10 minutes at 450°F., reduce heat to 350°F. and bake about 20 minutes more, or until the crust is browned. Serves 10.

GOLDEN RISOTTO

(color plate 6, top)

5 tablespoons butter or margarine	1½ cups chicken broth
½ cup chopped onion	Salt and freshly-ground pepper to taste
4 slices bacon, chopped	
1 cup rice	¼ cup grated Parmesan cheese
1 cup sliced carrots	Bacon curls and parsley for garnish (optional)
½ cup white wine	

In medium skillet melt 4 tablespoons of the butter. Add onion and cook until tender but not brown. Add bacon and cook until almost crisp. Remove all but 2 tablespoons fat. Add rice, stirring well to coat. Add carrots, wine and 1½ cups of the broth and bring to boil. Lower heat and cook, uncovered, for 15 minutes, or until liquid is absorbed. If necessary, add more of the broth. Season with salt and pepper. Stir in the remaining 1 tablespoon butter and the Parmesan cheese. Garnish with bacon curls and parsley. Serves 10 to 12.

SUCCOTASH

3 10-ounce packages frozen whole-
  kernel corn, or 3 cans
3 10-ounce packages frozen small
  lima beans

¼ cup melted butter
Salt
Pepper

Cook each vegetable according to package instructions. Combine the drained vegetables and add the butter. Add salt and pepper to taste. Serves 12 to 14.

AVOCADOS STUFFED WITH CREAM CHEESE

2 8-ounce packages cream cheese
⅓ cup sour cream
3 tablespoons lemon juice
¼ cup Mayonnaise (see page 154 for
  recipe)

2 tablespoons minced celery
2 tablespoons minced parsley
2 tablespoons chives or scallions
5 medium avocados, cut in half and
  pitted

Smooth the cheese with the sour cream, 1 tablespoon of the lemon juice and the mayonnaise. Stir in the celery, parsley and chives or scallions. Sprinkle the avocados with the remaining 2 tablespoons lemon juice. Spoon a little flesh out of each avocado cup and combine with the cheese mixture. Fill the avocados and chill. Serves 10.

AVOCADOS STUFFED WITH ROQUEFORT

Substitute 6 ounces Roquefort for the cream cheese and omit the celery. Spoon out half of the flesh from the avocados. Sprinkle the insides with lemon juice. Cut up the flesh and add to the Roquefort mixture. Proceed as for Avocados Stuffed with Cream Cheese. Serves 10.

HERB MARINATED NECTARINES

(color plate 7)

¼ teaspoon salt
1 tablespoon lemon juice
1 tablespoon cider vinegar
¼ cup oil

½ teaspoon crumbled chervil or basil
⅛ teaspoon freshly ground pepper
6 medium-sized nectarines, halved

In large bowl dissolve salt in lemon juice and vinegar. Stir in oil, chervil or basil and pepper. Add nectarine halves, toss lightly, cover and marinate, turning fruit once, for 30 minutes. Good served with cottage cheese and watercress. Serves 12.

WHITE LAYER CAKE
(WITH DELICIOUS CHOCOLATE FROSTING)

1 cup butter
2 cups sugar, sifted twice
2 teaspoons vanilla
1 teaspoon almond extract
3 cups cake flour

1 tablespoon baking powder
½ teaspoon salt
1 cup milk
6 egg whites, stiffly beaten

Cream the butter, adding the sugar gradually, until light and fluffy. Add the vanilla and almond extract. Sift the flour, baking powder and salt together 3 times. Add alternately with the milk to the creamed mixture, ending with flour. Beat until smooth. Gently fold in the egg whites. Line the bottoms of 2 greased 9-inch cake pans with waxed paper and divide the batter between the two. Bake at 375°F. for 30 to 35 minutes. Cool for 5 minutes and then turn out on a rack. Remove the paper and cool before frosting. Serves 8 to 10.

DELICIOUS CHOCOLATE FROSTING

3 ounces unsweetened chocolate
1½ cups sifted confectioners' sugar
1 cup cold water

3 egg yolks
4 tablespoons soft butter

Melt the chocolate in a double boiler. Remove from heat. Add the sugar and water and blend. The mixture will become quite stiff. Gradually add the egg yolks and stir well after each addition. The frosting will become soft and glossy. Add the butter and mix well. If the frosting is too soft to hold well on the cake, chill for a short time. Yield: enough frosting for the tops and sides of two 9-inch layers.

FORK-FOOD

Chicken Curry
Lamb Potato Casserole
Chutney
Eggplant in Foil
Baked Tomatoes with Mushrooms
Coleslaw with Red Onions
Blueberry-Grape Compote with Kiwis
Tiny Cupcakes

CHICKEN CURRY

2 4½-to 5-pound chickens	2 to 4 tablespoons curry powder
2 stalks celery with leaves	2 to 4 teaspoons lemon juice
6 to 8 medium-sized onions	1 banana, sliced
2 tablespoons salt	4 eggs
¼ cup butter	2 cups light cream
4 apples, peeled and coarsely chopped	Condiments
6 tablespoons flour	Rice
2 cups white seedless raisins	

Put the chickens in a large pot with water to cover. Add the celery, 2 of the onions, cut up, and 1½ teaspoons of the salt. Simmer until tender, about 1 hour. Remove from broth and, when cool enough to handle, remove the meat and cut into bite-sized pieces. Return the skin and bones to the broth. If the liquid has reduced too much, add a cup or two of water. Simmer, covered, for 30 minutes. Cool the broth, strain and remove the fat. All of this may be done well in advance. When ready to put the curry together, sauté the remaining onions, chopped, in some of the fat from the chicken broth or in butter. Add the apples. Add the flour and stir until the flour is lightly browned. Add 6 cups chicken broth, the raisins, and 2 tablespoons curry powder, stirring constantly. Continue to stir and cook until thickened. Add 2 teaspoons lemon juice, ½ tablespoon salt and the banana. Beat the eggs and cream together and add with the chicken. Adjust the seasoning, adding more curry, salt and lemon juice to taste. Serve as soon as hot. Condiments should be on the delicate side such as grated hard-cooked eggs, minced chives or scallions, grated coconut, crumbled crisp bacon, chopped peanuts, and always chutney. (See page 154 for a list of suggested condiments.) Serve with rice. Serves 16.

LAMB POTATO CASSEROLE

5 pounds lamb, cut into bite-sized
  pieces
16 medium-sized potatoes, peeled and
  sliced thick
1½ pounds onions, thickly sliced

1½ teaspoons salt
½ teaspoon pepper
3 to 3½ cups water or part broth
2 tablespoons chopped parsley

Remove any fat from the meat. Put a third of the potatoes in the bottom of a Dutch oven or other heavy pot. Add half the meat and onion and half the salt and pepper. Repeat. Put the last of the potatoes on top. Add the water and simmer, covered, for about 1 hour, or cook in a 350°F. oven for about 1 hour. Shake the pot a few times to prevent sticking. Make sure the lamb is tender. Add more water, if needed. Add the parsley for the last 15 minutes of cooking. Serves 14.

EGGPLANT IN FOIL

4 to 5 pounds eggplant
¼ cup olive oil
1 teaspoon salt

¼ teaspoon pepper
2 teaspoons lemon juice

Peel the eggplant and cut into cubes. In a heavy pan, sauté in the oil for 2 to 3 minutes. Transfer to a piece of foil, scraping in all the oil from the pan. Add the salt, pepper and lemon juice. Seal. Steam for about 15 to 20 minutes. Serve in a vegetable dish. Serves 10.

BAKED TOMATOES WITH MUSHROOMS

1 loaf day-old bread (unsliced, if
  possible)
2 pounds mushrooms, chopped
1 14½-ounce can chicken broth
1 small clove garlic, crushed
2 onions, minced
2 teaspoons salt
1 teaspoon paprika

1 teaspoon thyme
⅛ teaspoon hot pepper sauce
¼ cup flour
1½ cups seasoned bread crumbs
6 tablespoons butter
1 5-ounce can water chestnuts,
  coarsely chopped
14 medium-sized tomatoes

Trim the crusts off the bread and cut into ¼-inch cubes. You will need about a quart. Toast them lightly in a 300°F. oven until light tan, stirring so they toast evenly. Simmer the mushrooms in the chicken broth with garlic, onion, salt, paprika, thyme and hot pepper sauce for about 15 minutes. Thicken with the flour, made into a paste with cold water. Simmer and stir until the mixture thickens slightly. Add 4 tablespoons of the butter and stir until the butter melts. Add the croutons and water chestnuts and let cool. Cut the tops off the tomatoes, scoop out the centers and turn upside down to drain. Sprinkle the insides with 1 teaspoon salt, fill with the mushroom mixture, top with a few bread crumbs and dot with the remaining 2 tablespoons butter. Bake at 350°F. for 20 to 25 minutes until well heated through and tomatoes are soft but not mushy. Serves 14.

COLESLAW WITH RED ONIONS

1 2-pound head of cabbage, shredded
2 large red onions, sliced thin
½ to ¾ cup Lemon French Dressing
  (see page 155 for recipe)
2 tablespoons chopped fresh dill, or
  1 tablespoon dried

1 tablespoon caraway or celery seeds
  (optional)
Lemon juice
Salt
Pepper

Combine the cabbage and onion in a large bowl. Mix the dressing with dill and add the seeds, if you wish. Adjust seasoning, adding lemon juice, salt and pepper to taste. The dressing should taste strongly of lemon and be quite spicy. Pour over the salad and toss very thoroughly. Chill. Serves 10.

BLUEBERRY-GRAPE COMPOTE WITH KIWIS

(color plate 7)

¼ cup sugar
¼ cup water
½ teaspoon grated lime peel
¼ cup lime juice

2 pints blueberries
1 pound seedless grapes, halved
3 kiwi fruit, peeled and sliced
  crosswise

In small saucepan over medium heat stir sugar, water and lime peel until sugar dissolves. Remove from heat and stir in the lime juice. Cool. In bowl combine blueberries and grapes. Add the lime syrup and toss to mix. Cover and stir occasionally, chill well. Just before serving, garnish with kiwi fruits. Serves 8.

TINY CUPCAKES

Prepare Loaf Cake. (See page 57 for recipe.) Drop rounded tablespoonfuls of batter into greased 2½-inch cupcake pans. Bake at 375°F. for 15 minutes, or until a pick inserted in center comes out clean. Remove from pan to rack and cool. Yield: 36.

FORK-FOOD

Vegetarian

Salted Nuts
Soybean Chili
Onion Tart
Potato Salad with Cherry Tomatoes
Celery Salad
Green Salad
Deep Dish Blueberry Pie

SOYBEAN CHILI

1 pound dried soybeans
5 cups water
1 large onion, chopped
1 large green pepper, chopped
1 tablespoon oil

1 16-ounce can tomatoes, broken up
2 tablespoons ground cumin
2 tablespoons chili powder
1 teaspoon salt
¼ teaspoon pepper

In large Dutch oven soak soybeans in water overnight, or bring to boil, cook 2 minutes, cover, remove from heat and let stand for 1 hour. Bring to boil, cover and simmer for 1½ hours, or until just tender. Meanwhile, in skillet sauté onion and green pepper in oil until tender. Stir into bean mixture with tomatoes, cumin, chili powder, salt and pepper. Cover and continue cooking for 1 hour, or until beans are tender. If a thicker chili is desired, uncover for the last 30 minutes and cook until as thick as desired. Serves 8.

ONION TART

Pissaladière

5 cups chopped onion
5 tablespoons chopped parsley
2 cloves garlic, crushed or minced
1 teaspoon salt
2 tablespoons butter

2 tablespoons olive or vegetable oil
2 9-inch pie shells
1 pound Swiss cheese, grated
3 tomatoes, peeled and sliced

Sauté the onion, parsley, garlic and salt gently in the butter and oil until onion is transparent but not browned, about 10 minutes. Bake the pie crusts in a 350°F. oven for 15 minutes. Remove, cool slightly and pour in the onion mixture. Cover with the grated cheese and top with tomato slices. Bake for 30 minutes at 350°F. Cool and chill. You may serve at room temperature, if you wish. Serves 12.

POTATO SALAD WITH CHERRY TOMATOES

2 pounds potatoes, boiled
1 box cherry tomatoes
1 medium-sized onion, sliced thin and
    separated into rings
1 green or red sweet pepper, seeded
    and sliced thin

¾ cup French Dressing (see page 155
    for recipe)
Soft lettuce (Boston or Bibb)
2 hard-cooked eggs, sliced
2 tablespoons minced chives or
    parsley

Peel the potatoes and slice thin or cube. If the tomatoes are tiny, leave them whole; if not, cut them in halves. Put into a bowl with the onion rings and peppers. Pour ½ cup dressing over and refrigerate for several hours. Drain and put into a bowl lined with lettuce. Place the eggs over the top and sprinkle with chives or parsley. Pour the remaining ¼ cup dressing over and toss at the buffet. Serves 10 to 12.

CELERY SALAD

2 heads celery
¼ cup Lemon French Dressing (see
    page 155 for recipe)

2 tablespoons Mayonnaise (see page
    154 for recipe)
1 tablespoon prepared mustard

Wash the celery thoroughly under running water but do not pull the heads apart. Trim off any wilted leaves and trim the roots. Slice thinly crosswise through leaves and roots. Place in a shallow bowl. Combine the dressing with the mayonnaise and mustard. Blend thoroughly and pour over. It should cover the celery. If it doesn't, add a little more dressing. Let marinate for a number of hours or overnight in the refrigerator, stirring once or twice. Serves 6 to 8 (depending on the size of the celery heads).

GREEN SALAD

2 heads Boston lettuce or 3 heads
   Bibb
1 bunch watercress
2 large heads Belgian or 1 head curly
   endive

20 nasturtium blossoms and some
   leaves (if available)
½ to ¾ cup French Dressing (see page
   155 for recipe)
Minced chives or scallions (garnish)

Break the lettuce into small bite-sized pieces. Wash the watercress thoroughly, remove tough stems and cut up the leaves. Cut the Belgian endive into rounds or break the curly endive into small pieces. Place in a salad bowl. Wash the nasturtiums, cut some of the leaves into strips and add to the greens, saving the blossoms for the top. Chill until ready to serve. Pour dressing over the top and toss. Garnish with the chives or scallions and nasturtiums. Toss at table. Serves 10.

DEEP DISH BLUEBERRY PIE

3 pints or 3 9-ounce packages frozen
   blueberries
1 cup sugar
3 tablespoons flour
2 teaspoons grated lemon peel
1 tablespoon lemon juice

½ teaspoon cinnamon
¼ teaspoon salt
2 tablespoons butter
1 9-inch pie crust
Vanilla ice cream (optional)

Pick over fresh blueberries; thaw, if using frozen. Combine blueberries, sugar, flour, lemon peel and juice, cinnamon and salt in a 1½-quart casserole, dot with butter. Roll out pastry and cut to fit top of dish. Cut slits in pastry and pinch edge. Place over blueberry mixture and bake at 425°F. for 35 minutes, or until lightly browned. Serve with ice cream if you wish.

FORK-FOOD

Guacamole Dip
Crackers, Crudités
Lamb Curry, Indian Style
Chutney and Condiments
Near East Bread (pita)
Ham Ring
Stuffed Summer Squash
Grated Carrot Salad
Cherry Pie

GUACAMOLE DIP

2 medium-sized ripe avocados, pulp mashed
2 tablespoons fresh lemon or lime juice, or to taste
2 scallions, chopped fine
¼ cup canned green chili, chopped
½ teaspoon salt

Mix all ingredients thoroughly. Taste and adjust seasonings. Serve with crackers or raw vegetables. Serves 8.

LAMB CURRY, INDIAN STYLE

4 pounds lamb, cut into 1-inch cubes
3 tablespoons butter
4 large onions, chopped
1 clove garlic, minced (optional)
1 teaspoon salt
¼ teaspoon cayenne pepper
3 tablespoons curry powder
1 quart broth, or part water
3 tablespoons grated coconut
3 apples, peeled, cored and diced
1 large ripe banana, sliced
½ cup cream
¼ cup cornstarch
1 egg, beaten with 1 tablespoon milk or water
Rice
Chutney

Sauté the lamb in butter, stirring to brown evenly. Add the onion and the garlic, if you wish. Cook for 3 or 4 minutes more while stirring. Season with salt, cayenne and curry powder. Add the broth and simmer, covered, for 40 minutes. Add the apple, banana and simmer for 10 minutes. Add the cream mixed with cornstarch and simmer 5 minutes more. Bring to a boil and stir in the egg. Turn off the heat; the egg should leave streaks. Serve with rice and chutney. Other condiments may also be served (see page 154 for list). Serves 10.

HAM RING

(color plate 2)

2 pounds ham, coarsely ground
1 cup bread crumbs
1 pound pork, coarsely ground
1 cup milk
2 eggs, slightly beaten

1 cup chopped nuts (any kind)
2 1-pound jars or cans spiced or
    pickled peaches, drained and
    juice reserved

Combine the ham, bread crumbs and pork. Mix the milk with the eggs and add the nuts. Stir into the ham mixture. Stir in 1 cup of liquid from the peaches; blend well. Divide into two 3-pint ring molds. Bake at 350°F. for about 70 minutes. Cool slightly; unmold onto a platter and surround with the peaches. The center of the molds can be filled with a cooked vegetable, such as peas or French-cut green beans. Serves 12.

STUFFED SUMMER SQUASH

5 small crookneck squash
1 teaspoon salt
¼ teaspoon pepper
½ cup chopped onion
1 clove garlic, crushed
6 tablespoons butter

¼ teaspoon Worcestershire sauce
Pinch of cayenne
3 cups soft bread crumbs
¼ cup grated Parmesan cheese
2 tablespoons diced pimento

Wash the squash thoroughly. Steam, covered, in salted water for 35 to 40 minutes, or until tender. Remove and let cool. Cut off the ends, then cut in half lengthwise. Scoop out the seeds and pith. Season the squash with ½ teaspoon of the salt and the pepper. Arrange in a baking pan. Sauté the onion and garlic in butter until the onion is transparent and tender. Add the Worcestershire sauce, remaining ½ teaspoon salt and the cayenne. Toss with the bread crumbs, cheese and pimento. Fill the squash shells with this mixture and bake at 425°F. for 20 minutes or until the crumbs are brown. Serves 10.

GRATED CARROT SALAD

3 pounds carrots, scraped
3 tablespoons orange juice or
    1 teaspoon frozen concentrate
Grated peel of 1 orange

2 teaspoons lemon juice
2 to 3 teaspoons sugar
1 teaspoon salt
Lettuce

Chop the carrots in a processor or grate by hand. Combine with the remaining ingredients except the lettuce. Adjust seasoning. Serve in lettuce cups or on shredded lettuce. Serves 12.

FRESH CHERRY PIE

Pastry for a 2-crust 9-inch pie
4 cups sour red cherries
1 cup sugar

3 tablespoons minute tapioca
1 teaspoon lemon juice and/or almond
    flavoring

Line a pie plate with the pastry. Stem and pit the cherries and sprinkle with the sugar. Let stand for 1 hour. Drain and toss any juice from the cherries with the tapioca. Add flavoring and taste for sweetness. Stir in the cherries and pour into the pie shell. Cover with top layer of pastry, crimp edges and slash the top in several places. Or you may make a lattice top. Bake at 425°F. for 20 minutes, then reduce heat to 375°F. and bake 20 minutes. Serves 6 to 8.

CANNED CHERRY PIE

Substitute 2 1-pound cans pitted sour cherries, drained, for fresh. Use the liquid to mix with 2 tablespoons cornstarch and proceed as for Fresh Cherry Pie (omitting its tapioca).

FORK-FOOD

Crudités with Seasoned Salt
Cassoulet
Shrimp Curry
Chutney
Saffron Rice
Green Bean and Bean Sprout Salad
Irish Coffee Ice Cream
Drop Ginger Cookies

CASSOULET

2 pounds white or navy beans
5 cups water
1 teaspoon salt
1 onion, stuck with cloves
2 cloves garlic, crushed
1 bay leaf
Sprigs of parsley

½ pound Italian or other smoked pork
  sausage, cut up
½ pound salt pork, diced
1½ pounds roast lamb, boned
1 pound roast goose or duck (if not
  available, substitute pork)
Bread crumbs

Soak the beans in water for several hours or overnight. Cook in the same water with ½ teaspoon of the salt, onion, garlic, bay leaf and parsley for 30 minutes. Add the sausage and half the salt pork and cook 30 minutes longer. Drain, reserving the liquid (there is no need to strain the liquid). Place one-third of the beans in the bottom of a 4-quart casserole or earthenware dish. Push in part of the pieces of lamb and goose, duck or pork and half each of the sausage and salt pork. Cover with another layer of beans and remaining meat. Top with the last of the beans. Pour over 1½ cups of the reserved liquid and sprinkle with crumbs. Bake at 325°F. for 1 hour. If the beans seem dry, add more liquid; as they should be moist. Serves 10 to 12.

SHRIMP CURRY

4½ pounds small or medium-sized shrimp
1 small piece of ginger root
¾ cup grated coconut
2 onions, chopped fine
¼ cup butter
¼ cup flour

2 cups milk
1½ tablespoons curry powder
1 to 2 teaspoons salt
Grated lemon peel
2 tablespoons lemon juice
Rice
Condiments (optional)

Cook, shell and devein the shrimp. If the shrimp are large, cut through lengthwise. Soak the ginger, if it is dry; get a piece of fresh ginger root if possible. Simmer ½ cup coconut in water to cover for 15 minutes, strain and press out all of the liquid. Set the liquid aside and discard the coconut. Sauté the onion in butter until light brown. Stir in the flour. Add the milk, liquid from the coconut, curry powder, 1 teaspoon minced ginger root, 1 teaspoon of the salt and the lemon peel. Stir and cook until thickened and smooth. Add the shrimp, lemon juice and remaining ¼ cup coconut. Reheat. Add more salt and curry to taste. Serve with rice and chutney, and with other condiments if you wish. Serves 10 to 12.

SAFFRON RICE

2½ cups rice
¼ teaspoon saffron

1 teaspoon salt
5 cups water

Combine the ingredients in a large pot. Cover tightly and simmer for about 20 minutes. The rice should be tender and the liquid absorbed. Serves 10.

GREEN BEAN AND BEAN SPROUT SALAD

2 cups cooked French-cut green beans
1 pound mung bean sprouts or 1 16-ounce can, drained
1 cup chopped celery
¼ cup minced pimento or sweet red pepper

4 scallions, chopped fine
1 teaspoon sugar
¼ cup French Dressing (see page 155 for recipe)

Combine the beans with the celery, pimento and scallions. Add sugar to the French Dressing. Pour over the beans, toss and chill. Serves 6 to 8.

IRISH COFFEE ICE CREAM

1 to 2 quarts coffee ice cream
2 to 4 tablespoons instant coffee

4 to 6 tablespoons Irish whiskey

Soften the ice cream enough to spoon it into a chilled bowl. Quickly stir in the coffee and whiskey and freeze for at least 3 hours in a serving bowl. It will keep for weeks. Serves 6 to 12.

DROP GINGER COOKIES

1¼ cups butter
⅓ cup brown sugar
1½ cups molasses
1 egg, well-beaten
5 cups flour
2 teaspoons ginger

1½ teaspoons cinnamon
1½ teaspoons allspice
½ cup boiling water
4 teaspoons baking soda
½ teaspoon salt

Thoroughly cream the butter and sugar together. Add the molasses and the egg and beat hard. Sift 2 cups of the flour with the spices and stir into the creamed mixture. Add the boiling water and 1 more cup flour, mix well and refrigerate for 30 minutes. Sift the remaining 2 cups flour 3 times with the baking soda and salt. Mix into the batter and chill for at least 1 hour, or as long as overnight if you like. If chilled a long time, soften at room temperature before dropping by tablespoonfuls several inches apart onto a greased baking sheet. Bake at 350°F. for 8 to 10 minutes. Cool before storing in a covered container. Yield: 5 dozen.

FORK-FOOD

Platter of Marinated Vegetables
Chicken Potpie
Beef and Broccoli
Risi-Bisi Salad
Fruit Compote
Sand Tarts

PLATTER OF MARINATED VEGETABLES

(color plate 4)

1 pound green beans (about 2 cups)
4 large potatoes, cooked, peeled and diced
2 medium-sized yellow squash, sliced and cooked
4 medium-sized tomatoes, sliced
2 medium-sized red onions, sliced thin and separated into rings
¾ cup French Dressing (see page 155 for recipe)

Arrange vegetables on serving platter and sprinkle with dressing. Cover and refrigerate for at least 1 hour. Serves 10.

CHICKEN POTPIE

Filling:

1 5-to 6-pound chicken
1 teaspoon salt
¼ teaspoon pepper
1 cup chopped celery
½ cup chopped onion
3 sprigs parsley
¼ cup butter
¼ cup flour

Biscuit Top:

2 cups flour
½ teaspoon salt
1 teaspoon baking powder
6 tablespoons shortening
¾ cup milk

Put the chicken, salt, pepper and the vegetables into a large heavy skillet with water almost to cover. Simmer, covered tightly, for 1½ to 2 hours. Or you may steam it tightly wrapped in foil with the salt, pepper and vegetables and bake at 400°F. for about 2 hours. The cooking time depends on the age of the bird. Either way pull off the skin and remove chicken from the bones, keeping it in good-sized pieces. Return bones and skin to the pot, cover and simmer for 30 minutes. When ready to put the pie together melt the butter, stir in the flour and add about 2½ cups of broth slowly while stirring. Simmer until thickened. Put the chicken into a casserole and pour the sauce over, it should cover the chicken. If you do not have enough liquid you may add a little cream or half-and-half.

To make the biscuit top, sift the flour, salt and baking powder together. Cut in the shortening, add the milk and stir until blended. Knead briefly on a lightly floured board or cloth and form into about a 9-inch circle ¼ inch thick. Cover the casserole with the dough and pat it firmly around the edges. Bake at 450°F. for about 20 minutes. Serves 12 to 14.

BEEF AND BROCCOLI

(color plate 5)

¼ cup cornstarch	3 tablespoons oil
4 tablespoons soy sauce	1 clove garlic, crushed
2 tablespoons dry sherry	2 bunches broccoli, cut into small
3 teaspoons sugar	flowerets with 2-inch stems
1½ pounds round steak, cut across	1 cup shelled peanuts
grain diagonally into thin slices	

Mix well half the cornstarch, soy sauce, sherry, 2 tablespoons water and sugar. Add beef, toss to coat well. Cover and refrigerate up to 1 day. In a bowl mix remaining cornstarch, soy sauce, ½ cup water and set aside. In large heavy skillet heat oil until hot but not smoking. Add beef and sauté for 2 to 3 minutes. Remove with slotted spoon and set aside. Add garlic, broccoli and ¼ cup water. Bring to boil, cover and cook for about 3 minutes. Add beef, peanuts and cornstarch mixture and stir until sauce thickens.

RISI-BISI SALAD

3½ cups cooked rice	½ cup Mayonnaise (see page 154 for
2 10-ounce packages green peas	recipe)
4 scallions, minced	¼ cup French Dressing (see page 155
⅓ cup minced parsley	for recipe)
½ cup chopped celery	1 teaspoon lemon juice
	Lettuce

Combine the rice with peas, which have been cooked according to package instructions. Stir in the scallions, 2 tablespoons of the parsley and the celery. Mix the mayonnaise with French Dressing and lemon juice. Spoon onto the salad and toss gently. Chill. Place on a platter or in a salad bowl lined with lettuce. Garnish with the remaining parsley. Serves 10 to 12.

FRUIT COMPOTE

2 1-pound 4-ounce cans pear halves
2 1-pound 4-ounce cans peach halves
2 1-pound 4-ounce cans red plums

4 oranges, peeled and sectioned
½ cup kirsch

Put each fruit with its juice in a separate bowl and add a little kirsch to each. Each person can make his own compote with the fruits of his choice. Serves 12 to 16.

SAND TARTS

½ cup butter
2 eggs
1 cup plus 2 tablespoons sugar
1 tablespoon heavy cream
½ teaspoon vanilla

1½ cups flour
¼ teaspoon salt
1 teaspoon baking powder
½ teaspoon cinnamon

Cream the butter. Beat in 1 egg and 1 egg yolk, the 1 cup sugar, the cream and vanilla. Sift the flour, salt and baking powder together and stir into the butter mixture. Chill. Roll out thin and cut with a cutter about 1½ inches in diameter. Brush with beaten egg white and sprinkle with a mixture of 2 tablespoons sugar and the cinnamon. Bake at 350°F. for 5 to 7 minutes, or until the cookies are a pale gold. Yield: about 5 dozen.

FORK-FOOD

Mushroom Pâté
Crackers and/or Melba Rounds
Beef Stroganoff
Sole in a Casserole
Noodles
Tomatoes and Okra
Field Salad with Beets
Strawberry or Raspberry Ice Cream
Date Cookies

MUSHROOM PÂTÉ

1 pound mushrooms
1 bunch scallions (about 12 small),
   trimmed to 5-inch lengths
1 3-ounce package cream cheese,
   softened

2 eggs
¾ cup commercial bread crumbs
2 tablespoons dry sherry
1 teaspoon salt
⅛ teaspoon hot pepper sauce

Grease a 8 × 4 × 2-inch loaf pan, line with waxed paper, grease the paper and set aside. Wipe mushrooms clean (rinse only if necessary, and pat dry with paper towels). Cut mushrooms into quarters and scallions into 1-inch pieces. Chop fine in a food processor. Add remaining ingredients and process until smooth. If using blender, reverse procedure: add bread crumbs, eggs, cream cheese, sherry and seasonings until well blended. Alternately add mushrooms and scallions and whirl until blended. Spoon mixture into prepared pan. Set in pan with 1-inch hot water. Bake at 375°F. for 50 minutes, or until a knife inserted in center comes out clean. Remove from water and cool on rack for 10 minutes. Loosen edges and unmold onto a serving dish, discarding paper. Serve with crackers or melba rounds. Serves 8 to 10.

BEEF STROGANOFF

4 pounds beef fillet or sirloin
1½ teaspoons salt
½ teaspoon pepper
¼ cup butter
2 medium-sized onions, sliced

12 to 18 large mushrooms, cut up
½ cup beef broth or water
1 tablespoon flour
1 tablespoon Worcestershire sauce
1½ cups sour cream or yogurt

Cut the beef into narrow strips about 2 inches long, removing any excess fat. Sprinkle with salt and pepper. Brown in the butter in a heavy pot for 1 or 2 minutes, turning to brown evenly. Add the onion and mushrooms. Stir and cook 2 minutes. Add ⅓ cup broth, cover tight and steam for 10 minutes. Remove to a warm platter. Skim the fat from the liquid. Mix the flour and Worcestershire sauce with the remaining broth. Stir in and simmer for a few minutes. Remove from heat and stir in the sour cream or yogurt. Spoon the sauce over the beef. Serves 10 to 12.

SOLE IN A CASSEROLE

4½ pounds sole fillets
1 teaspoon salt
¼ teaspoon pepper
⅛ teaspoon paprika
5 tablespoons butter

¾ cup white wine
2 tablespoons minced onion
3 tablespoons flour
½ cup chicken broth

Pat the fillets dry and sprinkle with a mixture of salt, pepper, and paprika. Melt 3 table-spoons of the butter in a shallow casserole and lay the fillets in the butter; then turn them over so that both sides have a thin coating of the butter. Pour in the white wine. Heat the oven to 350°F. and bake the fish for 15 minutes. Meanwhile, in a sauce pan sauté the onion in the remaining 2 tablespoons butter until transparent but not browned. Stir in the flour and then gradually add the broth while cooking gently and stirring. Pour the wine and juices from the fish into this sauce, bring to a boil and then pour it back over the fish. Put under the broiler to heat and brown. Serves 10 to 12.

NOODLES

2 pounds noodles
5 scallions, minced (optional)
5 tablespoons melted butter or
   olive oil

¼ teaspoon white pepper
Salt (optional)

Cook the noodles in salted water until soft but not mushy, about 6 to 8 minutes. Drain. Mix scallions with the noodles, if you wish. Stir in the butter or oil, pepper and adjust salt to taste. Serves 10 to 12.

TOMATOES AND OKRA

2 pounds small fresh okra or 3
   10-ounce packages frozen
½ cup olive oil
4 onions, coarsely chopped
2 cloves garlic, peeled and chopped
1 29-ounce can tomatoes

1 teaspoon salt
¼ teaspoon pepper
1 teaspoon ground coriander
Lemon wedges (optional)

Trim tops from okra. Heat oil in large skillet and add onion and garlic. Cook gently until tender. Add okra and cook, tossing lightly, until slightly browned. Add remaining ingredients, except the lemon. Cover and simmer for about 45 minutes, or until okra is tender. Serve with lemon wedges, if you wish. Serves 12.

FIELD SALAD WITH BEETS

1½ pounds field salad, part arugula, if
   available
1 1-pound can whole small beets

⅓ cup French Dressing (see page 155
   for recipe)

Wash and dry the salad gently and break into bite-sized pieces. Drain the beets and rinse in cold water. Add to the salad and toss with the dressing. Serves 10.

STRAWBERRY ICE CREAM

1 to 2 quarts strawberry ice cream

2 to 4 packages frozen strawberries

Soften the ice cream enough to spoon it into a chilled bowl. Thaw the berries and puree in a blender or processor. Quickly stir the cold puree into the ice cream. Spoon it into a serving bowl and refreeze for at least 3 hours. This will keep for weeks. Serves 8 to 16.

RASPBERRY ICE CREAM

Substitute raspberries for strawberries in Strawberry Ice Cream You may strain the puree to remove seeds, if you wish.

DATE COOKIES

½ pound pitted dates
⅓ cup water
¼ cup sugar
1 teaspoon lemon juice
½ pound chopped almonds
½ cup butter

1½ cups brown sugar
1 egg
2 cups flour
¼ teaspoon salt
½ teaspoon baking soda

Cut the dates into pieces and cook in a saucepan with the water, sugar and lemon juice for 5 minutes. Cool. Add the almonds to the date mixture. Cream the butter, sugar and egg together. Sift the flour, salt and baking soda together and stir into the butter mixture. Chill this dough thoroughly. Roll the chilled dough into 2 rectangles of about 9 × 10 inches and ¼ inch thick on a floured board. Spread the date filling not quite to the edges of each rectangle and roll up like a jelly roll. Cut each in half, wrap in waxed paper and chill overnight. Each roll will be about 1½ inches in diameter. Cut slices ¼ inch thick and bake at 350°F. on a greased baking sheet for about 8 minutes. You can freeze the dough for later use. Yield: about 100 cookies.

FORK-FOOD

Stuffed Celery

Chicken Fricassee with Mustard

Shish Kabobs

Kasha

Broccoli Puree

Bean Sprout Salad

Build-Your-Own Sundae

STUFFED CELERY

2 heads celery
½ pound Roquefort or blue cheese

½ pound butter, or 1 8-ounce package
   cream cheese, softened
Worcestershire sauce

Pull the head of celery apart, trim the bottom and the leaves and scrape the stalks. Leave the small pieces whole but cut the others into about 3-inch lengths. Split them lengthwise if the stalks are very heavy. They should be easy to handle. Combine the cheese and butter or cream cheese, blending thoroughly. Add Worcestershire sauce to taste. Fill the celery, not too full. Chill until the filling is firm but not hard. Serves 12.

CHICKEN FRICASSEE WITH MUSTARD

2 6-pound chickens (fowls acceptable),
   cut up
6 tablespoons prepared mustard
2 teaspoons salt

30 small potatoes or 15 large, peeled
   and cut in half
1 cup sour cream
Minced parsley

Put the chickens in a pot with 2 rounded tablespoons of mustard per cup of water, using sufficient water almost to cover the chickens. Add the salt, cover, and simmer until tender, about 1½ to 2 hours, depending upon the age of the fowl. About 30 minutes before you plan to serve, add the potatoes. Add more salt and mustard to taste. Turn off the heat and

140

stir in the sour cream. (If you like a really heavy sauce, thicken with flour after the potatoes are done.) Sprinkle with parsley. Serves 16.

SHISH KABOBS

1 6-to 7-pound leg of lamb, boned	3 to 4 tomatoes, quartered
1 cup grated Bermuda onion	3 small Bermuda onions, quartered
½ cup olive or salad oil	24 mushrooms caps or small
1 tablespoon salt	mushrooms
2 tablespoons red wine	3 green peppers, seeded and cut into
1 teaspoon oregano	1-inch pieces
½ teaspoon freshly ground pepper	8 slices bacon, cut into 2-inch pieces

Cut the lamb into 1-inch cubes, trimming off any fat or membranes. Mix the grated onion with 2 tablespoons of the oil, the salt, wine, oregano and pepper. Rub this mixture into the meat until well coated on all sides. Refrigerate for 8 to 24 hours. When ready to make the kabobs, prepare the vegetables and bacon. Thread the meat and vegetables on the skewers, using mushrooms on the ends of the skewers and alternating in an attractive color pattern. Add the rest of the oil to the marinade and brush some over the kabobs and baste as they cook. Broil on one side until brown but not crusty and turn to brown the other side. Total cooking time is about 10 minutes. Serves 10 to 12.

KASHA

3 tablespoons oil	Dash of pepper
1 egg, slightly beaten	Dash of nutmeg or cinnamon
2 cups kasha	½ teaspoon salt

In large skillet heat the oil. Stir the egg into the kasha. Add to skillet and sauté over medium heat for 3 minutes, or until golden. Add pepper, nutmeg or cinnamon and salt and enough boiling water to cover kasha by 1 inch. Cover and simmer for 20 minutes, or until tender, stirring several times.

BROCCOLI PUREE

2 large bunches broccoli or 4	¼ teaspoon pepper
10-ounce packages frozen	1 teaspoon lemon juice, or
¼ cup butter, melted	⅛ teaspoon nutmeg
1 teaspoon salt	

Trim broccoli stems. Cook stems of broccoli in boiling water or steam until almost tender. Add tops and cook 5 minutes more. If using frozen broccoli, follow instructions cooking a few extra minutes. Put into a processor or blender with butter, salt, pepper, lemon juice or nutmeg. If you used fresh, add 1 or 2 tablespoons of cooking water from the broccoli. Reheat. Serves 8 to 10.

BEAN SPROUT SALAD

6 slices bacon
½ cup rice vinegar
¼ teaspoon pepper
1 teaspoon sugar

3 pounds fresh bean sprouts, or 3
   1-pound cans
6 scallions, chopped fine
2 tablespoons minced pimento

Fry the bacon until crisp. Remove to paper towels. Mix the vinegar, pepper and sugar with ¼ cup bacon drippings. Put the bean sprouts in a bowl. Drain, if using canned sprouts. Add the scallions and pimento. Pour the dressing over, toss and top with the crumbled bacon. Serve at room temperature. Serves 12 to 14.

BUILD-YOUR-OWN SUNDAE

Place 2 or 3 kinds of ice cream in cold bowls. The amount depends on the number of guests; count on 1 quart for 4 to 6 people. Have a number of dessert sauces on the table in separate bowls. If you wish, have a few garnishes such as chopped nuts, coconut, sprinkles or whipped cream.

FORK-FOOD

Liverwurst Pâté
Thin Rye Bread
Baked Stuffed Fish
Chef's Salad California Style
Broccoli with Cream
Cucumber Mold
Grasshopper Pie

LIVERWURST PÂTÉ

2 beef bouillon cubes
3 tablespoons boiling water
2 tablespoons brandy
1 envelope gelatin

1½ pounds liverwurst
¼ cup sour cream
2 tablespoons butter or margarine,
  softened

In small bowl dissolve bouillon cubes thoroughly in the boiling water. Add brandy. Cool and sprinkle on gelatin. When softened, place over hot water until gelatin dissolves. Heat liverwurst, add sour cream and butter and stir until blended. Add gelatin mixture and beat until smooth. Turn into oiled deep bowl. Cover and chill for several hours or overnight. Turn out on serving plate. Serve with thin dark bread or crackers. Serves 10 to 12.

BAKED STUFFED FISH

1 6-pound fish (whitefish, sea bass,
  lake trout or bluefish)
2 teaspoons salt
¼ teaspoon pepper
½ cup chopped onion
1 cup chopped celery
4 tablespoons butter

3 cups bread crumbs, or 2 cups
  crumbs and 1 cup poultry stuffing
¼ cup minced parsley
1 tablespoon fresh dill, or 1 teaspoon
  dried
¼ cup boiling water
2 teaspoons lemon juice
Lemon wedges

Leave the head and tail on the fish. Wash and pat dry. Sprinkle inside and out with half the salt and ⅛ teaspoon pepper. Make the stuffing. Sauté the onion and celery in 2 tablespoons of the butter until transparent but not brown. Add the remaining salt and pepper, the crumbs, parsley and most of the dill. Fill the fish and close the pocket with poultry pins or toothpicks. Brush the fish with 2 tablespoons melted butter mixed with the boiling water and lemon juice. Place the fish on a piece of foil or cheesecloth in a roasting pan (to facilitate taking it out when done). Sprinkle with the remaining dill. Bake at 350°F. for 45 minutes. Baste with pan drippings. Serve with the lemon wedges. Serves 10 to 12.

CHEF'S SALAD CALIFORNIA STYLE

1 head lettuce, broken into bite-sized pieces
1 bunch watercress
1 pound young spinach leaves
6 oranges, sectioned
1 cup slivered celery
1 cup slivered scallions
3 cucumbers, peeled and sliced thin
6 small tomatoes, peeled and quartered
1½ cups slivered ham
1 cup French Dressing (see page 155 for recipe) and/or other dressing

Combine the various greens and place the other ingredients in separate bowls. Serve the dressing on the side. Provide small bowls, if you have them, rather than plates. Each guest makes his own combination. Especially attractive served on a salad bar. Serves 10.

BROCCOLI WITH CREAM

2½ bunches broccoli
1 teaspoon salt
½ teaspoon pepper
1 clove garlic (optional)
¼ cup browned butter
½ cup cream

Trim the ends of the broccoli, break into flowerets, and scrape the lower part of the stems with a vegetable peeler. Steam on a rack for about 10 minutes, or until tender. Place in a warm bowl and sprinkle with salt and pepper. If you want the garlic, grate it into the butter. Brown the butter, add the cream, and pour over the broccoli. Serves 10.

CUCUMBER MOLD

4 large cucumbers, peeled and cut up
1½ teaspoons salt
½ teaspoon pepper
1 tablespoon sugar
3 scallions, cut up (green part and all)
¼ cup coarsely chopped parsley
2 tablespoons chopped fresh dill, or 1½ teaspoons dried
2 envelopes gelatin
½ cup cold water
½ cup Mayonnaise (see page 154 for recipe)
¼ cup sour cream or yogurt
½ teaspoon Worcestershire sauce
Sprigs of fresh dill or parsley (garnish)

Puree the cucumbers with the salt, pepper and sugar for a minute in a processor. Add the scallions, parsley and dill and process until smooth. Soften the gelatin in water. Heat and stir until dissolved. Stir into the cucumber mixture. Chill but do not let it set. Combine the mayonnaise with sour cream or yogurt and Worcestershire sauce. Stir into the cucumber mixture and taste for seasoning. Pour into a 1½-quart mold and chill for about 4 hours until set. Garnish with fresh dill, if available, or you may use parsley. Serves 10.

GRASSHOPPER PIE

2 envelopes gelatin
1 cup sugar
⅛ teaspoon salt
½ cup cold water
6 eggs, separated

½ cup green crème de menthe
½ cup white crème de cacao
2 cups heavy cream, whipped
2 9-inch baked pie shells
Additional whipped cream and shaved
    chocolate (optional)

In top of double boiler, mix together gelatin, ½ cup of the sugar and salt. Stir in water. Place over boiling water, stirring until gelatin is dissolved. Beat egg yolks slightly. Pour a small amount at a time of hot gelatin mixture into egg yolks and mix well. Put back over boiling water and cook, stirring occasionally, until mixture is consistency of unbeaten egg whites. Beat egg whites until foamy. Gradually add remaining ½ cup sugar and beat until stiff. Fold gently into gelatin mixture, then fold in whipped cream and mix lightly until blended. Pour the filling into the baked pie shells. Chill until firm. If desired, top with whipped cream and shaved chocolate. Serves 12.

PROCEDURES FOR COOKING AHEAD

Here is a play-by-play plan for buffet dinners to use as examples of the cook-it-ahead technique. A suggested procedure is given for each category for you to study.

SEMI-BUFFET

(See page 37 for menu)

Day before

Soup

Herbed Tomatoes (place
on serving platter)

Morning of

Cauliflower and green beans
cleaned and cut up. Refrigerate

Several hours before

Roast beef

Bake and stuff potatoes

15 minutes to 1 hour before

Heat soup

Heat potatoes

Cook vegetables

Fill fruit tarts (put on a platter)

Just before

Pour soup into tureen

Arrange food on platters
and serving dishes

Place entrée on serving table
on hot tray (except tomatoes)

HOT BUFFET

(See page 72 for menu)

Cook ahead and freeze

Pot Roast

Brownies

Day before

Chicken Breasts in Foil

Casserole of Green Beans

Tomato Aspic

Blue Cheese Dressing
(put in serving bowl and cover
and refrigerate)

Chill consommé

Morning of

Boil, peel and mash potatoes

Prepare watercress
(keep crisp in plastic bag)

Skin and bake peaches

Several hours before

Heat pot roast

Defrost brownies
and arrange on serving plate

Unmold Tomato Aspic
onto serving plate and re-refrigerate

Put consommé in cold bowls,
sprinkle with parsley
and refrigerate

15 minutes to 1 hour before

Heat mashed potatoes;
add butter and stir

Put chicken packages in oven

Heat Casserole of Green Beans

Garnish salad

Garnish peaches

Just before

Arrange Pot Roast on platter

Thicken gravy
and pour into gravy boat

Arrange chicken breasts
on serving dish

Place food on serving table

COLD BUFFET

(See page 110 for menu)

Cook ahead and freeze

Slice and salt cucumbers

Cookies

Day before

Poach or steam salmon

Green Sauce

Pâté

Morning of

Macaroni Salad with Ham

Glaze salmon

Raw Vegetable Salad

Macedoine of Fresh Fruit
(arrange in serving bowls,
cover and refrigerate)

Several hours before

Defrost cookies
(arrange on serving plate)

Dress cucumbers

15 minutes to 1 hour before

Dress vegetable salad

Garnish salmon platter

Just before

Place food on serving table

FORK-FOOD

(See page 140 for menu)

Cook ahead and freeze

Chicken Fricassee

Ice Cream (buy and keep frozen
until ready to use)

Day before

Shish kabobs

Sauces for ice cream sundaes

Morning of

Kasha

Broccoli Puree

Bean Sprout Salad

Make cheese stuffing for celery

Several hours before

Heat Chicken Fricassee

Stuff celery

Cook bacon for salad

15 minutes to 1 hour before

Heat Kasha

Heat Broccoli Puree

Dress Bean Sprout Salad

Broil Shish kabobs

Put out sauces for sundaes
in serving dishes

Just before

Place food on serving table

Put out ice creams

SALAD, DESSERT AND BEVERAGE BARS

THE SALAD BAR

Making your own salad from ingredients on a salad bar is very different from helping yourself to an already-made dinner salad from the buffet. The salad bar is on a different table where guests can take their time building a salad and not have to hurry without delaying the self-service at the buffet. The wider the selection the more pleasure there is in choosing your favorites and especially in avoiding your dislikes. Salads may be eaten first, last or with the meal.

In arranging the bar choose a variety of items from the following list and offer several salad dressings.

Always have a bowl of greens; tomatoes, sliced cucumbers, chopped celery, whole baby or sliced beets, carrot sticks or grated carrots, chopped or sliced green peppers, mushrooms, sliced fennel, sliced zucchini, sliced kohlrabi, cut or whole green or ripe olives, sliced or quartered hard-cooked eggs, chopped slivered onions, chopped scallions, diced cheese, sliced or diced cooked potatoes and cottage cheese.

Garnishes: Croutons, crisp bacon bits, grated cheese, minced chives, chopped parsley, grated hard-cooked eggs, fresh herbs, and sesame seeds.

Salad Dressings: In addition to olive oil and vinegar, French, Italian and Blue Cheese, you may wish to have Mayonnaise, Thousand Island or Lorenzo.

THE DESSERT BAR

If you have room for it, a dessert bar will provide a fitting and dramatic climax to a meal. Everyone likes a break between the entrée and dessert and everyone likes to choose his own.

On the bar, one can often construct one's own dessert. Making a sundae is a novelty at dinner. You may offer a choice of ice creams, a number of sauces and, perhaps, a few toppings such as chopped nuts, sprinkles, coconut and whipped cream. Various cut-up fruits can be made individually into a macedoine; a selection of stewed fruits in separate bowls allows you to make a compote to your taste. Piles of fresh fruit on a platter surrounding a mound of confectioners' sugar make a handsome display. Guests may choose to take several desserts from the tempting table.

Desserts present no great difficulty on the buffet. It is wise to serve fruit for the calorie-conscious in addition to a richer sweet for the fortunate few.

THE BAR BAR

If you have a bar in your house, you need no advice on the service of an aperitif or cocktails. If you decide to serve wine with your dinner, put the bottles and glasses at the end of the buffet and also a pitcher of ice water. No other beverage is appropriate to the meal.

SUMMARY

APPETIZERS when served in the living room with the aperitif should be small and easy to eat. If served with the meal they're frequently served cold so that they may be waiting at the table. Also hot soup in a tureen is a good first course.

FISH like most seafood, is easy to serve and eat at a buffet, if it has been boned. The unforgivable sin is to overcook it.

POULTRY being everyone's favorite, there are many recipes for help-yourself dishes from bite-sized pieces to huge turkeys carved on the buffet.

MEAT is the main dish entrée on many buffets. It is versatile, appearing in casseroles, stews, with sauces and as roasts that may be carved in the kitchen or on the buffet.

BREADS AND ROLLS are available in bakeries and even in supermarkets. Some appropriate breadstuffs are listed in the menus. Whole-wheat and health breads are recommended for vegetarian meals.

DESSERTS "make the end most sweet." In addition to the homemade sweets, fruits of some sort should be offered for the prudent.

VEGETABLES AND SALADS when fresh and crisp-tender, are a delight. Mix and match colors and textures. Meal salads are ideal for luncheons and a popular choice at a buffet dinner. Salads should be sparsely dressed if on a plate with an entrée. A salad bar is recommended. A list of dressings follows.

APPENDIX

SUGGESTED CONDIMENTS FOR CURRY

*A selection of these condiments should be served with
every curry.*

Chutney
Hard-cooked eggs, chopped
Chopped peanuts or walnuts
Chopped onion
Chopped scallions

Grated coconut
Chopped apple
Crumbled crisp bacon
Sliced banana
Raisins

SALAD DRESSINGS

On a salad bar you may wish to offer several kinds of dressings. Salad recipes contain suggestions for an appropriate dressing. Changing the herb flavors to suit your taste leads to a great variety in salads.

MAYONNAISE

1 egg
½ teaspoon dry mustard
½ teaspoon salt

¾ cup salad oil (small part olive)
2 to 3 tablespoons lemon juice or
vinegar

Break the egg into a blender or processor. Add the mustard and salt. Set the machine at the lowest speed and add oil slowly. Add vinegar or lemon juice to taste. Lemon mayonnaise is good with seafood. Yield: 1 cup.

RUSSIAN DRESSING

1 cup Mayonnaise (see preceding
  recipe)
½ cup chili sauce
½ cup catsup
2 hard-cooked eggs, chopped

2 teaspoons prepared mustard,
  preferably Dijon-style
1 tablespoon minced scallions, chives
  or onion
1 tablespoon India relish

Mix the mayonnaise with the other ingredients and chill. Reseason to taste.
Real Russian Dressing has 2 tablespoons caviar added just before serving!

FRENCH DRESSING

¼ cup vinegar
1 teaspoon salt

¼ teaspoon pepper
¾ cup olive oil

Put the vinegar in a bowl and stir in the salt and pepper. If you like a tart dressing, make
it 2 parts oil to 1 part vinegar. Use cider, wine or herbed vinegar. Add the oil and mix
thoroughly.

LEMON FRENCH DRESSING

Proceed as for French Dressing, substituting lemon juice for vinegar.

HERBED FRENCH DRESSING (VINAIGRETTE)

Add ½ teaspoon dry mustard and 1 teaspoon *each* tarragon, basil and chervil and 2 teaspoons minced chives or scallion to French Dressing.

ITALIAN DRESSING

Proceed as for French Dressing, adding ¼ teaspoon oregano and 1 clove garlic, crushed.
You may use ¼ teaspoon garlic salt instead of the garlic.

DESSERT SAUCES

On a dessert bar, you may wish to offer different kinds of dessert sauces. They are appropriate for ice creams, puddings, and some fruits.

CHOCOLATE FUDGE SAUCE

3 ounces unsweetened chocolate
¼ cup butter
1½ cups confectioners' sugar

9 tablespoons evaporated milk
Dash of salt
½ teaspoon vanilla

Heat all the ingredients, except vanilla, together in a double boiler. When the chocolate is melted, mix well and simmer gently for 30 minutes, stirring occasionally. Add vanilla and serve warm over ice cream. This sauce is fudgy, thick and delicious. Yield: about 1½ cups.

MOCHA SAUCE

When the chocolate has melted, add 3 tablespoons instant or freeze-dried coffee to Chocolate Fudge Sauce. Yield: about 1½ cups.

COFFEE SAUCE

3 eggs
¼ cup sugar

1 cup strong hot coffee

Beat the eggs with the sugar. Add the hot coffee. Cook and stir until thickened. Yield: about 1½ cups.

CARAMEL SAUCE

1 cup sugar
1 cup boiling water

2 tablespoons lemon or orange juice (optional)

Melt the sugar and cook, while stirring, until brown. Remove from the heat and add the boiling water. Simmer and stir for 5 minutes. Flavor if you wish with the lemon or orange juice. Yield: about 1½ cups.

BRANDY HARD SAUCE

½ cup butter slightly softened
1½ cups confectioners' sugar

3 tablespoons brandy

Cream the butter and gradually beat in the sugar and brandy. Chill slightly. Yield: about 1 cup.

RUM SAUCE

¼ pound butter
1 cup superfine sugar
⅓ cup rum

2 egg whites, beaten stiff, or ½ cup heavy cream, whipped (optional)

Melt the butter, add the sugar and stir until the sugar is dissolved. Remove from heat. Add the rum and stir. If you want a fluffy sauce fold in the beaten egg whites or whipped cream. Yield: about 1½ cups.

JUBILEE SAUCE

1 1-pound 13-ounce can pitted Bing
  cherries
1 2-inch strip lemon peel

1½ tablespoons lemon juice
1½ tablespoons cornstarch
2 tablespoons water

Drain the syrup from the cherries. Add the lemon peel and juice to the syrup. Mix the cornstarch with the water and stir into the syrup. Cook until clear and thickened. Add cherries and continue cooking for 10 minutes more. Cool or add ¼ cup warm brandy, ignite and serve flambé. Yield: about 2½ cups.

PIE CRUSTS

Several varieties of pie crusts are offered here for matching with the different fillings given in the menus.

UNBAKED CRUMB CRUST

1½ cups graham cracker or zwieback
  crumbs

¼ cup sugar
½ cup melted butter

Mix the crumbs and sugar thoroughly with the melted butter. Press this mixture evenly on the bottom and sides of a buttered 9-inch pie plate. Chill for about 1 hour until firm.

GRAHAM CRACKER CRUST

In 10-inch pie plate mix well 1¾ cups graham cracker crumbs, ⅓ cup softened butter or margarine and ¼ cup sugar. Press firmly in pie plate. Bake at 375°F. for 10 minutes. Cool then freeze, if desired.

CHOCOLATE CRUST

Proceed as for Graham Cracker Crust substituting crushed chocolate wafers for graham cracker crumbs and omitting the sugar.

GINGERSNAP CRUST

Proceed as for Graham Cracker Crust substituting finely crushed gingersnaps for graham cracker crumbs.

INDEX

158